The World's my Oyster

Book 1

Daz Tait

Fortis
Publishing Services

First Edition 2019 Fortis Publishing Services

Cover art: Nathalie Cauvi

ISBN-13: 978-1-9163212-0-5

Fortis Publishing
Kemp House
160 City Road
London
EC1V 2NX

Dedication

This book is dedicated to my mum, Rona Tait, who has always been fully supportive of all of my adventures and to my dad, William Tait, who taught me that a man is only as good as his word and that if you ever say you're going to do something, you better get it done. Rest in peace Pops.

Acknowledgements

First, I must thank my family for always being one hundred percent behind me for over two decades of adventure since I left home and forged ahead on my own, aged eighteen. It has always been good to know that if it all went completely Pete Tong (wrong) then I would have somewhere to call home and I wouldn't starve to death on the streets. To my Uncle Gordon, a merchant seaman, who captivated my imagination with stories of the sea from a very young age and my grandmother Molly, who never missed a day without saying, "If I was a man, I'd have been a sailor." May they both rest in peace.

Thank you to Mrs. Moore, my high school biology teacher, who opened up the world of international literature to me in an apartheid South Africa and taught me that 'You are free to forge your own reality.'

To all the skippers and sailors who took the time to patiently teach me the art of sailing: thank you for providing me with the skills to make 'the world my oyster'. Special thanks to Captain Awesome (Andi Healey) and Ross Appleby, I learnt more from the two of you than all of the rest combined.

Mark Poyser, for taking the giant leap of faith and selling up to set sail with me aboard Hitrapia. It's a shame we didn't make it around together, but I respect the fact that he was willing to give it a go.

Thank you to the people of Sagres who helped me

in my time of need. There are way too many of you to thank individually but you know who you are. To the Atlantic Rally for Cruisers (ARC) and their workers, collectively known as the yellow shirts; your efforts to organise an incredible rally gave me my first real taste of the cruising lifestyle. The innumerable people I met throughout the Mediterranean and in the Caribbean, your kindness and hospitality were what made the trip so special. I promise to pass your generosity forward one day, even if it is just to help out another ocean vagabond washed up on my shore. A special thanks to the Mykonos Malakas, keep on charging boys.

A huge thank you must go to Ken Scott, my writing coach, who taught me the skills to be a proficient writer and helped me produce a story that I am very proud of. To Anne Kennedy, my editor, your advice and patience has been invaluable. My gratitude also goes to Nathalie Cauvi, for taking the time to hand paint the beautiful, unique covers for the whole trilogy.

Lastly, to Reinette Visser, the owner of Fortis Publishing, for taking me on as a client. I look forward to a long and successful partnership.

I never thought that writing about sailing around the world would actually be harder than circumnavigating, but take my word for it, it was. I hope you enjoy reading my books as much as I enjoyed writing them.

Follow my adventures

www.daztait.com

Table of Contents

Prologue

This tale starts in the little bay of Baleeira, on the southwestern tip of the Portuguese municipality of Sagres. It was neither the beginning, nor the end of this adventure, but in a way it symbolised a bit of both.

I'd arrived a week earlier, after three days of solo sailing in my thirty-five-foot Trident Warrior yacht, called Hitrapia, making my last stop on mainland Europe before sailing across the Atlantic. It was to be the first major leg in my bid to sail around the world.

It had been a brutal seventy-two-hour solo sail to get there, but I'd made it and I couldn't have been happier because I had been put to the test and passed with flying colours. Navigating through the Strait of Gibraltar - one of the busiest shipping channels in the world – as a solo sailor, meant that I only ever got to sleep for a maximum of ten minutes at a time.

Big ships move quickly and a quarter of a million-ton super tanker that's invisible below the horizon fifteen minutes before can loom over your little boat in no time. So, whenever the coast was clear I'd set my alarm and drift off into another world, jolting back to reality ten minutes later. I'd sit up, rub my eyes and scan the horizon. If all was clear I repeated the process, an exhausting way to spend seventy-two hours but the only option if I wanted to stay alive.

But I'd made it safely to the bay and taken up a mooring buoy for the week. Although a little rundown, Baleeria looked just like any other typical fishing port, with dozens of little boats moored in the shallows and the deeper water covered by a dozen mooring buoys for visiting yachts. I planned to be away from the boat for much of the day and the forecast indicated varying wind directions, so I figured it would be much safer to be on a buoy than anchored and the port captain assured me the mooring buoys were 'forte, forte' (strong).

I'd stopped in Sagres to catch up with friends from the Swiss summer camp that I worked at every year.

They were all surfers and hadn't stopped talking about how incredible the waves in the Algarve are, so I decided to check it out. On the morning of the fateful day that changed the course of my life, I ferried five of them and their surf gear to my boat and we set out.

Nicolau, me, Marta and Concha in the water

'Coffee anyone?' I enquired and five hands shot up. I left Nicolau, an experienced skipper in his own right, on the helm as I popped into the galley to boil some water.

Concha, an incredible surfer and all-round beach babe, joined me downstairs to help.

'This is going to be so cool, Daz. I have always dreamt of jumping off the back of a boat and surfing waves from the ocean side.'

'It's got to be way better than having to paddle through all the breaking waves first. Have boat, can travel,' I said, which made her smile.

'For eighteen months now you haven't stopped talking about how much you love this boat. I'm so happy we're getting a chance to sail on it together,' she said as she gave me a big hug, 'I'm so proud of you for following your dreams.'

Concha was my fellow water-sports instructor and we'd spent a couple of summers in Switzerland together teaching kids how to sail.

'Thanks sweetie. It's been a struggle to get here, but I made it in the end,' I replied, dishing out steaming mugs of coffee.

Nicolau and Concha getting their surf gear onboard

We sailed around the coast to Barranco Bay and anchored up a couple hundred metres offshore. To the envy of everyone in the line-up we paddled in and surfed our first wave without even getting our hair wet on the way there. We surfed for hours until we were all knackered and returned to the boat for lunch before sailing back towards the port where I attached Hitrapia to the same buoy I'd used all week. My friends were so delighted with their surfing and sailing adventure that they invited me ashore for dinner and we headed off to party. After our meal, we went to a bar for drinks and ended up in the local nightclub. I was having the time of my life, surrounded by good friends as we danced the night away. After eighteen months of preparing my own yacht, I felt like a bona fide skipper with the whole world laid out before me and life couldn't have been any better.

At 4am the party finished, and I headed back to the boat. When I arrived at the quay, I was irritated that I couldn't see my anchor light out in the bay. Only a couple of weeks before, I'd been up the mast and replaced the old anchor light with an expensive L.E.D. version and I was pissed off that it had apparently failed.

I gazed out to sea as I cursed the manufacturer under my breath and then surveyed the beach. My heart skipped a beat as something caught my eye. About two hundred meters away, suspended about ten meters above the sand, was a familiar bright light.

I shook my head and mumbled to myself. 'No, it's not possible.'

As my gaze fixed on the light, I forced myself to look lower. Below it, heeled at a forty-five-degree angle was the unmistakable shape of a hull I knew only too well. As the reality of the situation dawned on me, my heart almost jumped out of my chest. My body dumped adrenaline into my bloodstream as I took off down the beach like an Olympic sprinter. I arrived breathlessly, gasping in horror as I spotted the mooring buoy, rope and heavy chain all hanging from the boat's bow cleats. The other end should have been attached to a five-ton block of concrete on the ocean floor, but the chain had snapped and the swell had pushed Hitrapia up onto the beach and then receded with the tide to leave her high and dry. My legs buckled as I fell to my knees in shock, my brain struggling to compute what was going on. I couldn't believe what I was seeing. My beautiful yacht marooned on land with my entire world turned upside down.

With a heavy heart I forced myself to my feet and looked at my watch. It was only about three hours until the next high tide and the possibility of floating Hitrapia again.

With the help of Jesus, I set to work. No, I hadn't magically found religion in my time of need but I had woken up one of my friends, Jesus Rodriguez, sleeping in his camper van at the local dive school. I rowed three anchors fifty metres offshore and dug them into the ocean floor and as the tide returned, I tried to winch my floundering yacht back into deeper water but she wouldn't budge from where she was beached on the sand.

Over the next two days, with help from a salvage team of local fisherman, we tried everything we could to float her again. My friends and other volunteers worked in shifts and I worked forty-eight hours without sleep, as we emptied the tons of sand washed inside Hitrapia. As we cleared the last few shovels of sand it became clear why she wouldn't re-float. Sticking through the hull was the corroded remains of an old fuel tank, dumped on the beach. With the pressure of the waves, the rusty tank had acted like a gigantic tin opener and sliced a hole in the beam of the boat and subsequently split the hull open along its entire length.

Pablo, the big burly sea captain in charge of the salvage team, placed a hand on the nape of my neck. We had worked, shoulder to shoulder, trying to save her for more hours than I cared to recall.

'What the fuck Pablo,' I asked, 'what do we do now?'

He turned to me with a forlorn look in his eyes and stated, 'I'm sorry, my friend. She is gone.'

Pablo, the salvage team and my friends all gradually drifted away. They asked me to come with them back to port, but I told them I needed a little time on my own. I couldn't leave Hitrapia all alone, it was like abandoning an old friend.

Hitrapia

The wind picked up and tormented me as it howled along the beach in strong gusts. The waves pounded away at what was left of my beautiful boat, wedged in the sand. Hitrapia's stark outline sat at a precarious angle as she ground back and forth in the swell and I remember surveying my surroundings. With huge rocky boulders strewn in the ocean to my left and a cement pier way down the beach to my right all I could think to myself was what a shit place to die. I sat with my knees up to my chest, huddled in a salt-encrusted hoodie with a half-empty bottle of whisky in my hand, the only item to have survived the wreckage. Hitrapia, the most beautiful thing that I'd ever known. Not now... like my dreams, she was utterly shattered.

I had lost everything I owned and had no idea what the future held. With little money left in the bank and my passport confiscated by the maritime police so that I couldn't flee the country before disposing of the wreckage, life wasn't looking too good as I sat all alone, destitute in a foreign port with a broken heart. The unique odour of rotting vegetation you get on the seashore filled my nostrils and mixed with a smell that didn't belong there. It took an age for my exhausted brain to work out that the strange smell was diesel fuel and something inside me snapped. An overwhelming wave of misery engulfed me as I finally broke down and began to cry. I cried for all the things I'd sacrificed, shed tears for everything I'd lost. I ranted at the world for what could have been and screamed into the uncaring wind how unfair life was. But mostly, I mourned for my beloved Hitrapia, cruelly taken from me before she had a chance to fulfil her destiny.

I'd lost a loved one, but it felt like I'd lost my soul as my dreams of sailing around the world lay scattered all around me. That night I crawled into my tent on the beach, shipwrecked; a sailor's worst nightmare.

Chapter 1

Seize the moment

I'm not going to lie and say I always wanted to sail around the world. As a kid, I didn't dream of sailing the seven seas; no, I wanted to be a palaeontologist and search for dinosaur fossils. However, the thought of travelling to far-flung exotic destinations to discover wonderous new things always filled me with excitement.

I was born and raised in Johannesburg, six hundred kilometres from the ocean and pretty far away from any form of sailing culture. Still, I loved the ocean from a very young age. Some of my earliest memories are of Amanzimtoti on the South Coast of Durban. We spent almost every school holiday at the beach and my parents thought nothing of the seven-hour drive to get there. They'd collect us at the school gates on a Friday afternoon and we'd drive to Granny's apartment for a weekend visit. I played in the surf with my father and brother Craig from the time I was in nappies. I loved the way the sand felt between my toes and how beautifully cool and refreshing the saltwater felt on my skin. Every day at the beach was different, a new adventure, and you never knew what you might find washed ashore. I was fascinated with all the little creatures that scurried about and spent hours exploring the coastline and snorkelling in the rock pools and that cemented my lifelong love affair of anything to do with the sea.

Craig and me (I'm on the left)

I was entranced by the power of the waves and learned early in life to respect the ocean after being pulled out by a rip current at the age of twelve. It was just like every other day that summer. I'd got up at 6am and headed down to the beach for a swim, body surfing at my usual spot, when a freak set of large waves rolled in. The waves would have pounded me onto the beach so with no other option, I frantically swam towards them and dived to the ocean floor. They washed over the top of me and I resurfaced a few seconds later, but all that water had to return to the sea and it ripped my feet from the sandbank and took me with it. At first, I struggled against the current and swam with all my might to regain my footing, but to no avail, the ocean's power is incredible and I stood no chance. My father had always drummed it into my head that if I ever got caught in a rip current, I had to swim parallel to the shoreline and not against the current. I followed his advice and swam perpendicular to the mighty force that had taken hold of me, but it was no good. I was fighting a losing battle and kept getting swept out to sea. I tired quickly and began to tread water instead as the choppy ocean spray made it difficult for me to breathe. I tried to relax, but I could feel a rising panic each time I lost sight of the shore as I dipped between the rolling waves, coughing and spluttering as I swallowed seawater. Just when I thought all was lost, a surfer grabbed me by the scruff of the neck.

'You silly little bastard, what are you doing all the way out here?'

He plopped me on the front of his board and paddled the 100m back to shore, depositing me on the beach like a drowned rat. With his dire warning to respect the ocean ringing in my ears, I remained on dry land for the next week.

After that harrowing experience, it took a little time to get my confidence back in the water. Still, the only way I've ever known how to deal with fear is to confront it head-on. So I befriended some local lads, paid them in Granny's bacon sandwiches and they taught me the basics of how to bodyboard. After a couple of weeks, the sea and waves were something I no longer feared, but an incredible entity I learnt how to harness for pleasure.

The idea of sailing around the world started when I was around nineteen. I'd recently emigrated from South Africa to England and it was one of those beautiful, British summer days when all the pubs' beer gardens were full. My girlfriend at the time had previously introduced me to her best friend's brother, Mark, and we sat enjoying a pint together in the sun. Mark's a great character to hang out with and one of the funniest guys I've ever met. He always seemed to be on the move to somewhere new and exciting with adventurous tales to tell. If he wasn't off in his VW Campervan to Devon for a surf trip, then Mark was jetting off snowboarding for the winter season. With a mop of dreads and a happy go lucky outlook on life he'd have made a great hippy.

In between bouts of excessive drinking and taking the piss out of each other, Mark mentioned he was considering doing a Yachtmaster qualification so that he could sail the seven seas. I had no idea what being a Yachtmaster entailed, but the more we discussed it, the more excited and animated we became. What could be better than travelling around the world on a boat, exploring exotic lands and cultures, powered by nothing but the wind and your own strength? We would be proper adventurers separated from the usual tourists of the world and on a quest of personal discovery. We joked and laughed about it, but the seed of an idea had been planted in my mind. As the years rolled by, whenever the two of us met up, our conversations continued to centre around the idea of sailing around the world and we seemed fated to follow this journey together.

I put myself through an Economics degree at university and headed to the Alps for a snowboarding season. Through good luck and great timing, I secured a job at Aiglon College and when the snow season finished, I started work as a residential house tutor in the boarding school. I knuckled down and completed a distance learning course to become a secondary school mathematics teacher.

But the idea of sailing was never far from my mind. During the school holidays I headed back to the UK to complete sailing courses and race in the Solent, continuing to build my confidence and inching my way towards the goal of becoming a competent skipper. I wanted to sail my own boat around the world.

My blissful life in Switzerland ended abruptly when a new headmaster stepped in and changed the school's boarding system and passed me over for a teaching promotion. To become a fully qualified teacher, I needed to teach full time and that opportunity had evaporated. So, I applied for a new job and secured one in a private boarding school in Surrey, just south of London. A positive consequence of my move back to England was that I was once again in constant contact with Mark. We agreed to buy a yacht together and after crunching the numbers there was a lot of money to save. We needed £20,000 each to put towards a boat, then the same again to live off. I gave myself four years to get it but little did I know how tough the challenge of teaching full time and living on a shoestring budget would be.

School term started and life became hectic. As any new teacher will tell you, the first two years are brutal. There's so much to learn, so many resources to produce and skills to develop. I worked non-stop and hardly saw a yacht or had time to think about adventures as I focused on surviving each teaching week.

My new school had introduced the International Baccalaureate Qualification, and everybody was under severe strain. Aside from teaching I also coached a sports team, participated in outdoor activities on weekends and gave my life and soul to the school. As I liked to say, 'they got their pound of flesh and a pint of blood too.'

Surrey, like London, is expensive and the single room I rented cost me £600 a month, a third of my salary. I just seemed to haemorrhage money and by payday, I had very little to show for working like a dog. At that rate my savings target would take me the best part of twenty years to complete, but Surrey is in the British countryside and with forest parks dotted all around I hatched a plan to save myself a fortune. I purchased a white panel van, stripped out the old oil-stained interior, built a platform for a double mattress and designed a perfect little home for myself. I left my accommodation in Surrey at the beginning of March and moved into the back of my Citroen Dispatch mini campervan, parking in the forest every night, close to nature, and only a short drive from school.

I learnt a lot from my time living in a van. I learnt to survive with next to nothing and how little I needed to be happy, content in a small yet uncluttered space. I awoke in the forest every morning to birdsong and every night I could escape the reality of school, heading back to the hills and revitalising my soul with the beauty of nature. With shower facilities and free food at the boarding school, it worked well and on weekends, I always had a friend's couch to sleep on if I drank too much to drive.

Dispatch Dave, my camper van home

With the onset of winter, life in the van became untenable. The cold, short days caused everything inside to become permanently damp and returning to a freezing, wet, metal cocoon each night after a hard slog at work began to get me down. Fortunately, I found a colleague who was willing to rent me his attic room in South London for the winter months. For £50 a week I had a draughty winter nesting hole, but it was so cheap I could continue to save £1000 a month. I was on a mission now and to save more money, I bought a bicycle and started to cycle the 40km round trip to school every day. Each morning I left at 5-30am in the freezing cold, dark and dreary days of winter. It was tough, but I knew I had to keep my eye on the prize. Every litre of diesel I saved brought me one small step closer to owning my yacht and the freedom I so craved. I also loved a challenge and pushed myself to cycle as fast as I could. Rain, sleet or snow, nothing stopped me on my bike. The worse the weather, the more exhilarating I found the ride as I raged against the elements and fought my way through the unceasing London traffic jams.

During my last two years as a teacher I spent every spare minute researching cruising yachts and scouring the internet for suitable boats. Mark had spotted a Bavaria 45, fully equipped for a sailing circumnavigation. It met most of our specifications, even though it was a little bigger and more expensive than we'd planned for. Since Mark had done the hard work finding the boat, it was my job to call the owner and get some more information. The call started off cordially as he passionately went through every modification he'd made to the yacht. Gary was sixty-five years old and spoke with devotion for his beloved craft. He answered all my questions with ease and things were sounding very positive until I asked him why he was selling. The phone went silent and then Gary began to cry. It took him a few minutes to compose himself before the whole story came out.

'I've been building and modifying this boat for the last fifteen years. For fifteen years I've spent every minute of my free time down at the boatyard getting her ready to sail around the world. My wife would come too, polishing and cleaning, and she kept me supplied with sandwiches and cups of coffee.'

He stalled again. I heard him blowing his nose.

'We talked about where we would sail, all the exotic places we had dreamed of going to for donkey's years. Mary was as keen and enthusiastic as I was and we couldn't wait to go, Son.'

He explained he'd been retired six months and been putting the final touches on the boat while he counted down the days until his wife retired too.

'I remember crossing out the number 90 and then 89 on the calendar. We were like two small children counting down the days to Christmas.'

I sensed there was a 'but' coming as Gary paused for breath.

'I crossed out day 88 and shouted through to my wife in the kitchen that it wasn't long to go.'

He continued. 'Mary didn't answer which I thought was a little unusual,' he laughed, 'she was never short of a word or two. I walked through to the kitchen and found her lying on the floor.'

'No,' I said, 'I'm so sorry!'

'My beautiful wife of forty-five years had suffered a major stroke.'

He broke down in tears again as I waited on the end of the line.

'She'll be bedridden for the rest of her days and our dream of sailing around the world together is shattered, it will never happen.'

After he'd composed himself, he asked about my plans. I told him that in twelve months of saving every penny, I'd be ready to set off around the world.

The next thing he said was one of the most heart-breaking things I'd ever heard, but it also inspired me to change my outlook on life.

'Young man, my life is over, my wife's life is over too. If we are lucky, we might spend the next ten years looking at the same four walls, but that was not the way we planned it. I kept thinking that I needed more time to get the boat ready and more money before I could go on the adventure I'd dreamt about all my life.'

My mouth was dry, I couldn't find any words to comfort him.

'Needing money was just an excuse son. The wind is free, the seas and oceans have no tolls. I had the boat; it was paid for ten years ago, but we waited and waited. Just go, while you are young and as soon as you can!'

That conversation sealed my fate. After I put the phone down, I promised myself that whatever happened, after one more year of work required for me to become a fully qualified teacher, I'd head to sea. As Gary had said, it was now or never. I didn't want to make the same mistake so many do, sustaining themselves for decades on a future dream that just passes them by.

In the end, we didn't buy Gary's boat but his words affected me profoundly.

I gave him a courtesy call to say the boat wasn't for us and just before I hung up, he told me not to forget about what he had said.

'I won't,' I replied, 'your advice meant a lot to me.'

'Good,' he said, 'seize the moment Son, seize the moment.'

Chapter 2

Letting go

My final year of teaching flew by. At the end of my penultimate term, I walked into the headmaster's office and handed in my resignation. The school broke up for the summer holidays and my four years of teaching in Surrey came to an end. It had been an emotional roller-coaster; I was leaving everything I knew behind me and was about to step into a totally new world. Although I embrace risk, this was an extreme step even for me. As the summer holidays loomed, I spent many sleepless nights as an irrational fear of the unknown gripped me. I lay awake for hours and wondered what the hell was I doing. Why was I giving up the safety of a good job that offered me loads of career progression? Why was I sacrificing a decent salary and three months of paid holiday a year to go sailing? Couldn't I just be happy with what I had instead of reaching into the unknown? All these thoughts paled in comparison to the agonising question of what to do about May, the love of my life.

May and I had met at Sheffield University. We had similar interests and partied together when we weren't studying. There was something captivating about her spirit and I always gravitated towards her. The fact that she is a beautiful little redhead whom I could pick up with one arm helped too. In her presence the world seemed brighter and filled with hope and joy for the future. Over the next decade, we saw each other regularly at parties and reunions, but the timing was never quite right. Whenever I was single, she had a boyfriend and vice versa, but that all changed one summer.

Every year since graduating from university, I'd worked in a summer school in Switzerland. May, not only beautiful and intelligent but creative too, was attending a prestigious London University to study documentary film making. She was at a loose end over the summer and we needed somebody to make the summer camp's video that year so she applied for the job and I made sure she got it.

The first week of camp, I took every opportunity to be around her. I helped her move into her studio and drove her around campus, inviting her to all the parties and social events that, work permitting, I could get her to. One night, as we sat together and watched a movie at my best mate Dibble's apartment, I had this barely controllable desire to envelop her in my arms. I couldn't think about anything other than her and it was driving me insane. The movie flew by - not that I can remember any of it - and May said her goodbyes and headed home. I couldn't take it anymore; I was besotted with the girl. It felt like I was going to explode with frustration and I sprinted out of the flat and caught her on the way down the stairs.

I was breathing hard. 'May, this is difficult for me to say, but if I don't get it off my chest, I'm going to go crazy,' I stammered as my heart pounded in my chest. 'I like you, no, no, that's not right, what I mean to say is that I really like you and I've felt this way for as long as I can remember.'

If I'd thought about what I was going to say to her instead of charging out on the spur of the moment, I might have come up with something better, but I was committed and ploughed on.

'I need to know how you feel about me before my head explodes.'

May stepped back and gathered her thoughts.

After carefully weighing up her words she responded, 'I'm sorry Daz, there's too much history here, we're just friends. I've never felt like there could be anything more.'

I hadn't really known what to expect and felt both disappointed and relieved at the same time. The sexual tension I'd been feeling for weeks drained away as I gave May a big smile and shrugged my shoulders.

'Well at least now you know,' I said, 'I've been wanting to tell you that for years.'

She smiled. 'That was a courageous thing to do Daz,' she replied, as she stepped forward and gave me a big hug, 'it takes a lot of courage to tell somebody how you feel. Thanks for letting me know.' We continued to work alongside each other and I tried to block out any thoughts of the two of us getting together, but with little success. My heart still managed to betray me, skipping a beat every time I saw her. After almost a month of torture, summer school was drawing to a close and I'd pretty much given up hope. Then, on our last night out in Switzerland, May walked straight up to me in the pub.

'I've been considering this for ages now,' she said as she stood on her tiptoes, placed both hands on my shoulders, leaned into me and gave me the most mind-blowing kiss of my life. My body responded immediately as years of frustration and longing poured out of me in a wave of passion. When we finally separated, May took my hand, turned on her heels and simply said, 'take me home.'

Complicated by our previous relationships with mutual friends, we got off to a rocky start, but ten years of friendship and an overwhelming physical attraction helped us to overcome all obstacles.

Within a month I'd uttered the three most dangerous words, I LOVE YOU, and meant it. For the first time in my life, I could see a future together with somebody whom I loved, but to be with May would mean kids and houses and embracing life in London. We had an incredible year of fun and adventures together, but deep down inside I knew that if I stayed in London the rest of my life was already mapped out for me. I'd get married, borrow a fortune and buy an outrageously overpriced shoebox to live in. We'd have children and I'd work my arse off to keep my head above water for the next forty years. After falling in love with May, it dawned on me that there was another love in my life: the boat I knew I had to buy. I didn't want to accumulate the useless trappings of a consumerist society, retire and totter around on a cruise ship until I had the good grace to die. I wanted a life full of adventure. I was in love with May, but I was still craving for that other love affair, the seas and the oceans that meant freedom. I wasn't ready to settle down just yet.

The Dalai Lama put it perfectly when asked what surprised him most about humanity. He said:

'MAN

BECAUSE HE SACRIFICES HIS HEALTH
IN ORDER TO MAKE MONEY.

THEN HE SACRIFICES MONEY TO
RECUPERATE HIS HEALTH.

AND THEN HE IS SO ANXIOUS ABOUT
THE FUTURE THAT HE DOES NOT
ENJOY THE PRESENT;

THE RESULT BEING THAT HE DOES
NOT LIVE IN THE PRESENT OR THE
FUTURE;

HE LIVES AS IF HE IS NEVER GOING TO
DIE AND THEN DIES HAVING NEVER
REALLY LIVED.'

I wanted to see the world while I was still young and energetic. I wanted to have amazing adventures before society sunk its claws into me and I became just another hamster stuck on capitalism's wheel. That wasn't too much to ask, was it?

May is wiser than I'll ever be and sensed this long before I ever did. I tried my best to talk her into coming sailing with me, painting the picture of exotic places and carefree days sailing on the seven seas. She knew that Mark and I were nearly at the stage where we were ready to invest in a decent boat and I tried to sell her a dream, my dream.

It was the one word I shouldn't have used. May explained that in her past relationships, she'd got stuck following her boyfriends' dreams and now it was time for her to follow hers. Her family, home and community were all in London and they always would be. After weeks of agonising indecision, I finally made up my mind. If I was going to live a life of no regrets, then I had to break up with her to follow my dream of circumnavigating the globe. Letting May go was releasing the final tether that bound me to the only way of life I knew and it was the toughest decision I've ever had to make. For a relationship to work, both people need to be moving at the same speed and in the same direction. That, sadly, just wasn't the case for the two of us. I will always hold May in the highest regard, and I apologise for the pain I caused her near the end of our time together. She deserves all the happiness in the world and I am glad she has found it. After our break-up, a vast sense of loss and heartbreak lingered for many months, but I was finally unencumbered and free to head to sea.

Chapter 3

The eye of the storm

Sailing - like most things in life - requires practice if you'd like to enhance your skills. You can learn all the sailing theory in the world from the comfort of your armchair. Still, no amount of studying can take the place of the practical, hands on experience you get on the water and the more time you spend out at sea, the more varied situations you encounter, building your confidence and ability to make the correct decisions when under pressure. For years I crewed on various vessels during the school holidays and was often astounded at the level of incompetence displayed by some of the self-proclaimed 'skippers' I sailed with.

I knew the sea could be a pretty unforgiving mistress and I didn't want to be yet another sailor with all the gear but no idea. So, before buying a yacht, I decided it was imperative to get some ocean sailing experience. I did some research and found out that hundreds of sailboats set off across the Atlantic from the Canary Islands to the Caribbean around the end of November each year. This mass departure of yachts coincides with the end of the hurricane season in the North Atlantic. It's also the time when the trade winds start to blow from east to west across the ocean. Without the trade winds, no sailing yacht can cross the Atlantic Ocean's 3,000 nautical miles, a measurement of distance that requires a short explanation in order to understand how speed is calculated at sea.

Take a look at a world map. You will see it is crisscrossed with a lot of lines. The vertical ones, or lines of longitude, are known as meridians. They are thicker in the middle and taper to a point at either end, just like the segments in an orange. The horizontal ones are lines of latitude, splitting the earth from north to south and run parallel to each other. This means that each line of latitude is equidistant from the next and perfect for measuring distance. Some gifted mathematicians centuries ago calculated that the average circumference of the earth is about 40,000 kilometres. I say average because our world isn't perfectly round, it's actually an oblate spheroid with slightly flattened poles, which basically means it's been a bit squashed. To all you Flat Earthers out there, the poles are the only flattened bits on the planet, so you're more than welcome to go and live there, you plonkers!

Now imagine you travelled from the North Pole to the South Pole. You'd have journeyed halfway around the world or 180 degrees of a circle. Cartographers (a cool word for map makers) started at zero degrees for the Equator and split the earth into the Northern and Southern Hemispheres with 90 degrees of latitude in each. They further divided each degree of latitude into sixty parallels and called those minutes. Half the world's perimeter of 20,000 kilometres, divided by 180 degrees of latitude, then divided by the 60 minutes found in each degree gives you a total of 1.852 kilometres, or one nautical mile.

In theory, the longer a yacht's hull length, the quicker it can move through the water. One knot is the speed you travel if you cover one nautical mile per hour. On a thirty-five-foot cruising yacht like Hitrapia, four to five knots is the average speed. A little boat like Hitrapia could sail on average 110 nautical miles a day and take four weeks to cross the Atlantic. On a fifty-footer, six to seven knots would be the norm, covering 150 nautical miles a day - a three-week ocean crossing. To put that in perspective, it's about an eight-hour flight to cover the same distance by air which makes sailing sluggish by comparison.

I could have taken a quick flight to the Canaries but the whole point of the adventure was to gain as much sailing experience as possible so flying just wouldn't do. I searched through numerous crewing websites and found a fifty-foot yacht that was heading down that way. The boat was called Great Escape, a prophetic name indeed. It was sailing from Portsmouth in England to Las Palmas de Gran Canaria, a distance of 1,500 nautical miles and was leaving the UK at the end of August, only a week after I first saw the advert so I arranged a Skype interview to get a feel for what I was getting myself into. The skipper was a petit woman in her mid-thirties with short, curly blond hair and glasses, called Emma. She was quietly spoken and the polar opposite to the big, burly sea captains of my imaginations.

Nevertheless, with over twenty transatlantic voyages under her belt, she was an experienced sailor and quickly put me at ease. There is nothing worse than being stuck on a yacht with a captain whose abilities you don't trust when conditions turn rough. Even though I hadn't done much offshore sailing before, Emma could hear how serious I was about gaining experience and how willing I was to learn from her. For a nominal fee to cover food and fuel, I hopped on board Great Escape with four other crew members and my bona fide ocean sailing education began, aged thirty-one.

It was an uneventful and rather disappointing start to the voyage. We left Portsmouth in light winds that died within a day and we motored most of the way across the English Channel. Normally we would have waited for better wind, but that trip was a yacht delivery and the owner wanted the boat in Las Palmas within a fortnight. So, we fired up the steel spinnaker (a nautical term for the engine) and made good time. The wind conditions were still calm as we rounded Brest in north-west France and headed towards the dreaded Bay of Biscay. Biscay, situated off the coast of France and Northern Spain, has a fearsome reputation among sailors. Within the bay, the ocean's depth changes from four thousand metres to less than two hundred metres over a very short distance as the water approaches land. This underwater escarpment is known as the continental shelf and it thrusts the full power of the ocean towards the surface, creating turbulent, steep waves. When the effects of the continental shelf combine with the ferocious Atlantic gales that batter the European coastline in winter, monstrous waves are formed that can sink tankers. It comes as no surprise that insurance companies refuse to cover sailing yachts in this area any time after October.

My crewmates on board Great Escape in calm weather.
Florin, Scouse, Steve and Emma

We kept a watchful eye on the weather and the forecast looked fine, so Emma decided to go for it. The weather in Biscay is notoriously fickle and over the next thirty-six hours, the winds continued to increase. The new forecast showed a powerful low-pressure system (low pressure always brings wet and windy weather) forming over the Atlantic, racing across the ocean to meet us. By now we were too far from the safety of land to run for cover and our only option was to fight it out. This wasn't Emma's first rodeo. She knew what she was doing, positioning Great Escape well off the continental shelf and in the relative safety of the deep oceanic water. Following her clear and calm instructions, we battened down the hatches, strapped down everything that moved and reduced the sail area in anticipation of the violent winds to come. Less sail area means that the wind transfers less power to the boat and it's referred to as reefing.

From the western horizon loomed a giant black cloud, blotting out the sky. It rolled relentlessly onwards, looking more and more menacing as it approached. It was the first significant storm I had ever faced at sea and I felt trepidation and excitement in equal measure.

The wind continued to increase as it screamed through the rigging and the ocean swell reached a size I'd never seen before. With thunder and lightning flashes overhead, the stormfront hit us, heeling the boat to one side as we sped into the gloom. The howling winds drove horizontal rain and freezing sea spray, cutting visibility down to a couple of metres. Over the peak of every wave the yacht accelerated downhill and the sails flogged as they were shielded by the next rolling wave. As we rode up the face of successive waves, the sails cracked like a whip as they once again filled with wind and it was like riding on the back of a fifty-foot dragon, the most exhilarating roller coaster ride of my life. Throughout all of this, the boat forged ahead under the expert steerage of the skipper. Wrapped up from head to foot in my wet weather gear and attached to the cockpit with a safety line, I watched in awe as she battled the elements. With a look of grim determination on her face, she struggled to maintain her footing on the pitching deck, never wavering as she focused all her attention on breasting the next wave, hour after hour.

Imagine you are a little cork inside a giant washing machine, and you'll get an idea of what it's like to be in a gale. The waves threw me from side to side as the yacht fought to stay upright. Every movement had to be choreographed in time with the pitching and rolling of the deck and the occasional rogue wave would catch me unawares, bouncing me off an unforgiving surface and adding another bruise to my growing collection.

The ferocious storm we faced in Biscay

Conditions were brutal, but Emma's quiet competence filled the entire crew with confidence, extinguishing any of my doubts and I felt no fear. To get some rest, I wedged myself into my cabin and snoozed as best I could but the inside of the boat was so sticky from condensation that it was a relief to get back out into the elements to do my next watch.

Still, by the end of my three hours on deck, I was so tired that I welcomed my dank sleeping quarters again. This probably sounds like a nightmare, but within a day, I didn't notice the discomfort anymore. You can either fight it and hate every minute of it or accept that the conditions aren't ideal, acknowledge that they cannot continue that way indefinitely and just get on with it until things improve. I chose the latter. I'd be lying if I said I loved every minute of it, but I certainly enjoyed myself. We fought that storm for three days until the sun finally broke out in all its magnificent glory. It was the first storm I ever weathered at sea and I survived my baptism of fire. I'd found the unforgiving world of ocean sailing; a world where there are no excuses and poor decision making is quickly punished.

Watching Emma helm through the worst of that storm made me realise just how much I wanted to be a competent sailor, capable of standing up to whatever the ocean threw at me. Just like her, I wanted to be confident in my ability to look after myself, my crew and the yacht under my command, in all conditions. That storm cemented my fate. I was hooked and nothing was going to stop me from learning how to cross the world's vast oceans safely.

After nine days at sea we arrived in Lisbon, Portugal. I was delighted to be unaffected by seasickness, unlike another poor sod on the crew who had been throwing up over the side for days. He'd been unable to sleep, looked a pale shade of green and jumped ship the moment we docked. I couldn't blame him; it must have been an awful experience. Seasickness is brought on by the discrepancy between what your eyes see and your inner ears' balancing mechanism feels when you're rolling around on the ocean and it typically manifests itself when sailors go below deck. Everything inside looks normal to their eyes, but they are unable to see the horizon. At the same time, their ears are telling them that the world is still moving and this inconsistency between their senses makes them feel very ill. To this day I have never suffered from seasickness, but I've seen it prostrate many a sailor, rendering them utterly useless as they cling to the railings for days, consigning the contents of their stomachs to the fish following in the boat's wake.

To make sure that I didn't get too cocky, King Neptune still had one little trick left up his sleeve. During the voyage, I joked with the crew about how much I loved a good pint of Guinness. I like Guinness so much that a future goal was to hike 600 kilometres across Ireland from Dublin to Kerry, just because an Irishman once told me that the flavour improves the further west you travel across the Emerald Isle.

On docking, all the crew set off in search of a bar that sold the black and white nectar of the gods and it wasn't long before we found an Irish pub and sat down to enjoy a few pints. It had a been a tiring week and after a couple of drinks we decided to call it a night and head back to the boat, but when I stood up from the table, my world began to wobble. The Portuguese love to decorate their town squares with beautiful black and white mosaics and stretched out before me, as far as the eye could see, lay an undulating pattern of black and white tiled waves wending their way into the distance. I could still feel the roll of the boat beneath me as my ears hadn't yet become accustomed to being back on solid ground. At the same time, my mind knew the land shouldn't be moving but the tiled floor tricked my eyes into believing it was. As my brain worked overtime attempting to guide my deranged senses, I managed to stagger to a wall and prop myself up as another wave of vertigo hit me. I stared around in disbelief and then burst out laughing. The rest of my crewmates were also wobbling about like toddlers as they struggled to place one foot in front of the other, all afflicted with a dose of land sickness. We must have been hilarious to watch, providing loads of entertainment for the locals and tourists alike. There had never been a more apt time to break into song as we all began to sing, 'What will we do with a drunken sailor …'

The walk back to the dock was raucously funny and those two glasses of Guinness will go down as the most entertaining pints I've ever enjoyed.

Chapter 4

A mutiny

We arrived safely in Las Palmas a week later and I spent the next month attempting to secure myself another crewing position. A company called the Atlantic Rally for Cruisers (ARC) organises an annual transatlantic race. That's the reason why over three hundred yachts were docked in Las Palmas and there were hundreds of other vagabonds trying to hitch a ride on one of the ARC boats. I walked the docks for hours every day, making as many contacts as possible in the hope of securing a berth but competition was fierce. My evenings were spent in the dock bars chatting to the skippers of various boats, a tough job but somebody had to do it!

My efforts finally paid off. Peter, a salty old sea dog who resembled Doc from the cult movie, 'Back to the Future', offered me the last place available on his catamaran. Although there was something rather strange about Peter, I couldn't quite put my finger on what it was and hoped that once I got to know him better things would work themselves out. I'd looked for a crewing position for ages and pickings were slim, so I jumped at the opportunity and agreed to help Peter prepare his boat for the race.

Yachts undergo harsh conditions and extreme forces when sailing across oceans, so everything has to be in perfect working order before heading out to sea. We checked the mast, examined the rigging and serviced the engine. We cleaned the hull and completed a myriad of other tasks. For every one thing we fixed on Peter's yacht, we found another three things to keep us busy. The never-ending cycle of boat jobs seemed to go on forever.

The work was going well, and I enjoyed learning about yacht maintenance, but the more time I spent with Peter, the more I realised how downright peculiar he was. I'm a really outgoing guy and made dozens of friends in Las Palmas while searching for a skipper. My two nicknames at university were the 'Social Butterfly', because I talked to everybody and the 'Energiser Bunny', as I never ran out of energy to party. So dealing with an anti-social, grumpy old bastard was challenging. A decade of solo sailing had robbed Peter of his ability to interact with people, that's if he'd ever had any interactive social skills to start with. As time wore on, he really started to get on my nerves with his reclusive behaviour. When he did venture out, he expected me to spend all my spare time in his company and he became irate whenever I spoke to my other friends.

'We are a crew, Daz,' Peter would say to me every time we left the boat, 'We walk together. Talk together. Do everything. Together!'

For Larry, the other crew member on board, it was his first sailing voyage. He didn't know any better and followed Peter around like a puppy, but I was really struggling. Peter's attempt to try and control my behaviour on shore didn't sit well with me and after a fortnight I couldn't stand the man's company anymore. I had met many cool skippers on my rounds of Las Palmas, so I knew Peter's behaviour was weird. The coolest skipper of the lot was Andi, a solid ex-bodybuilder from Manchester that we affectionately nicknamed Captain Awesome. He was built like a brick shit house and cut an intimidating figure. The only thing stronger than his muscles were his opinions and he had one of those for just about every topic under the sun. Andi is well-read, intelligent and funny and I held him in high esteem. I also trusted his integrity and approached him for some advice.

'Hey, buddy, what's up? You don't look like your normal cheery self,' he asked as I joined him for a beer after stealing away from the boat.

'Mate, do you expect your crew to follow you wherever you go?'

'Hell no,' he replied, 'we'll be at sea together and in one another's pockets for long enough. A break from each other is as good as a holiday.'

'And what about when the boat jobs are done for the day?'

'When the work's done, the work's done. It's free time, baby!' he shouted out, startling the couple next to us as I burst out laughing, the first time I'd laughed in days.

'Peter's under the misguided notion that because I'm his crew member, he owns every minute of my day,' I confided in him.

'Daz, you are one of the friendliest and most outgoing guys I've ever met. You chat to everyone. Sounds like Peter is sucking the life out of you.'

'Yeah man, I'm a free spirit, my mission is to meet as many amazing people as possible. It's about drinking, socialising and generally being merry. I feel like a fucking prisoner in Peter's company.'

'Mate, if you can't stand the man onshore then sailing with him is going to be purgatory.'

'You don't have a spare locker I can stow away in do you?' I joked.

'I wish. I've got the boat owner and his mates for this crossing so we're full. But I'd have taken you in a heartbeat if I could.'

The next morning after Peter lectured me on how dishes should be washed, I'd had enough of the prick and started to pack up my gear. The old bugger must have thought I was heading out for the day.

'I haven't given you permission for any time off,' he said, 'where do you think you're going?'

I picked up my bag and threw it over my shoulder. 'I'm out of here for good you cantankerous old bastard, the thought of another day on this boat with you and I'll be throwing you overboard.'

I started to walk.

'You get back here this minute,' he screamed.

I couldn't believe what he'd just said, he was speaking to me as if I was a child.

'Who the fuck do you think you're talking to?' I yelled back at him, 'I'm leaving. Good luck. You're going to need it.'

I stepped off his boat for the last time and walked away as he shouted after me.

Granted, it wasn't the most auspicious moment to walk off a boat with only a couple of days left to go before the rally departed, but if you can't get on with somebody ashore, then you sure as hell aren't going to survive each other's company in the confines of a small boat on a long ocean passage.

I was back to square one and feeling pretty disheartened. It had taken me over a month to find my first berth, the rally left in two days and I was without a ride. It had been a disastrous morning but at least that evening was the ARC's final leaving party for the fifteen hundred people taking part in the transatlantic race. If it wasn't meant to be for me to cross the Atlantic with the ARC Fleet, then I was definitely going to go out with a bang and get up to loads of shenanigans at their final bash.

With free drinks, pumping music and lots of dancing with my friends, I hit that party hard. I was in my element and I must have looked like a total pimp, dancing on stage, surrounded by a bevy of beautiful women whom I'd met over my time on the island. During a little intermission from partying I was standing at the bar when a handsome looking chap in his 50's approached me. Impeccably dressed and confident, he introduced himself as Tony and offered to buy me a drink. The thought he may be gay crossed my mind.

'Cheers mate, but the drinks are already free,' I declined, 'and I'm not that way inclined. But seeing as I'm feeling so generous, how about I get you one.'

Tony burst out laughing, 'you've got the wrong idea, buddy. The drink was to be in payment for an introduction to those people you're dancing with, you seem to know everyone.'

We had a good laugh over my misunderstanding of the situation and drank a pint together. I liked Tony from the start; an open, friendly guy who was up for a good time with his mates. I hadn't met him yet as he'd only just arrived in port due to a delay with the delivery of his new catamaran. We chatted for a bit and I mentioned I'd walked off the cantankerous old bastard's yacht that same morning. After grabbing more drinks, we strolled over to chat to the rest of his crewmates. They were all good lads, so I happily helped to integrate them with the rest of the ARC participants and we partied into the wee hours of the morning.

As the night drew to a close and we said our farewells, Tony stumbled over, gave me his business card and asked me to meet him for coffee in the morning. I didn't think much of it, but I had nothing else to do so I agreed and we went our separate ways. The next morning, I felt as rough as a badger's backside, but I'd promised to meet him early so I dragged my hungover arse out of bed and made my way to the rendezvous.

Tony got straight to the point.

'Daz, before we met last night, I had the unenviable job of asking one of my friend's mates, the fourth crew member and the only guy I didn't know before the voyage, to pack his bags and leave my yacht.'

'What?'

'Yeah, it was the right thing to do because we had a big personality clash and I just didn't feel comfortable with him onboard.'

He took a gulp of coffee before continuing.

'I wasn't too bothered about filling his space. The other three lads are solid, but after meeting you last night, all the boys have unanimously agreed that we'd like to invite you to join us for the crossing.'

My jaw nearly hit the floor.

'I'd have asked you last night, but we were all too drunk. I wanted to discuss it with the crew in the cold light of day before making a final decision. What do you think?'

'What do I think?' I shouted, 'that's the best news I've heard all year.'

I jumped up to shake his hand and then gave him a huge bear hug instead. I was over the moon. I'd miraculously managed to find a second berth the day before the rally's departure by just being myself. My outgoing personality, which caused animosity with my previous skipper, was embraced by Tony and his crew. Tony, a wealthy man but generous to a fault, offered to cover all my expenses for the entire trip if I was willing to act as his first mate (the position of second in charge aboard a yacht). He'd sailed around the world a decade before on his first boat, but this trip was with his friends and they weren't experienced sailors so he could do with the help. That was it, I couldn't quite believe it. I'd just been invited to sail across the Atlantic on a brand new, two-million Pound Lagoon 560 luxury catamaran with a professional chef on board, and it was all for free. It was as if all my Christmases had come at once. Things were definitely looking up again as I skipped back to my hostel to collect my gear. As Metallica so eloquently put it, 'Forever trust in who you are and nothing else matters.'

We set sail the next day to the fanfare of three hundred boats leaving in close proximity, all destined for St Lucia in the Caribbean, 3,000 nautical miles across the Atlantic Ocean. It was exciting to be underway but still, my overriding emotion was one of relief at having found a berth just in the nick of time. Some of the wanderers I'd hung around with over the last two months in Las Palmas hadn't been so lucky, but they all came to wave me off. As they stood on the dock, waving and cheering, their selfless gesture brought a tear to my eye. It could have been me standing there, stranded on the quay, waving to all my friends as they made their way out on the adventure we'd all been dreaming of.

Las Palmas

The first two days of sailing were blissful. The weather was perfect with clear skies, fair winds and the sea rolled on all the way to an unbroken horizon. We sailed on a disk of dark, sparkling ocean below the dome of an azure sky. Two contrasting blues, both astounding in their all-encompassing splendour. On the first night we could still see a dozen boats, their navigation lights dotted all around us, but by the next morning, we were all alone, surrounded by nothing but water. I was amazed at how so many yachts, all heading towards the same destination, could all but disappear overnight. It was my first glimpse of how gigantic the world's oceans are.

The transatlantic crew: Steve, Tony, Alan, me and Locky

I spent the first couple of days getting to know the other crew. There was Tony, the flamboyant owner/skipper who I've already introduced. Steve, the co-owner of the yacht, who kept himself to himself. Alan, a retired engineer who could fix just about anything which came in very handy, as contrary to what you may think, more things seem to break on new boats than they do on old ones. He also had some sage advice for me which I promptly ignored. When I told him that I was going to buy my own boat, he turned to me and said, 'Don't be stupid, boy. Sail other people's yachts, it's much cheaper.'

Locky

And last, but not least, was Locky the chef, who cooked some of the best meals I've ever eaten at sea.

I spent the rest of my time familiarising myself with the yacht. It was unbelievable to be on a boat that was, in essence, a floating hotel. The Lagoon 560 had four double cabins, each one with enough space to walk around the king-sized beds. All the rooms were fitted with en suite facilities, called the heads in maritime jargon. On all of the yachts I'd sailed on previously, I was lucky if I got my own tiny bunk bed, no bigger than a coffin, and I'd always shared a toilet with everybody else on board. This boat was in a different league with a huge galley that could satisfy Gordon Ramsay. There was even a wine rack and a plasma screen television in the saloon. I'd hit the jackpot. Still, as I was to learn time and time again in sailing, every boat is a compromise of sorts and huge, thirty-foot-wide catamarans are no exception to the rule.

After two idyllic days, the weather turned and we were in for a storm. The trade winds switched from behind us and blew from a westerly direction in front of us. Sailing with the wind off the bow is called beating and I was just about to find out why. Single hulled vessels are designed to cut through the water and even though beating into the wind against the incoming waves can be uncomfortable, it is not unbearable. Catamarans, on the other hand, have two hulls that are connected together by a flat horizontal structure called a bridge deck. I'd never sailed a cat before and had no idea what to expect, but I was in for the worst forty-eight hours I've ever endured at sea.

As the wind picked up, the oncoming waves increased in size. What goes up must come down and every time we crested a wave, thirty tons of boat slammed into the ocean, battering the bridge deck with incredible power. The force was so great that each pontoon vibrated for a couple of seconds after the impact. It felt horrible to stand on a boat with a deck that was quivering like jelly, but that was nothing compared to the vile pounding that echoed through my cabin. When it was my turn to sleep, I lay down on my bed in dread, knowing the chances of catching a couple of hours shut eye were zero. Every twenty seconds, it felt like somebody was attempting to smash their way into my room with a sledgehammer as we pounded through the surf. Every few minutes, as we headed over an even bigger set of waves, I'd get airborne, hovering above my bed for a second before crashing down onto the mattress.

BOOM! BOOM! BOOM! A relentless bone-jarring percussion akin to being stuck in hell's foulest death metal mosh pit. All of this mayhem was compounded by Tony refusing to put any reefs in the mainsail. On every sailboat, you can change the area of the sail. Making the sail smaller is called reefing and our entire mainsail was out as we charged through the swell, driven along with all the sail up. The boat felt overpowered and right on the edge of being out of control. If you ask any sailor whether they've been scared at sea, and they reply with anything other than a resounding 'YES,' then they're either lying, stupid, or haven't done any ocean sailing with an overzealous skipper pushing his boat dangerously close to the edge.

I was crapping myself that first night of the storm, bouncing away on my bed as I contemplated my own mortality. I thought there was no way that the hull could possibly hold up to the continuous abuse it was being subjected to and I was convinced it would split apart. Even if the boat did survive, we were likely to get dismasted as the fury of the storm increased. The only positive things I could think of was at least we had two engines if we lost the mast, and we weren't too far away from Las Palmas to get a helicopter rescue if it all went wrong. In a fatalistic gesture, I said my prayers for the first time in two decades, plugged my ears and attempted sleep with one thought jarring inside my brain. At least if I perished, I'd die in the attempt of fulfilling my dream.

The weather raged on for another day until the continuous pounding gradually subsided as the wind veered behind us with the passing of the storm front. Tony - not for want of trying - hadn't managed to destroy the yacht. We all survived and I had a newfound respect for boat builders and the tensile strength of glass-reinforced plastics. Tony, for all his bravado, was a nice fellow but had little idea of how to sail his boat. I had asked him a dozen times, in the interests of safety, to slow the boat down but it had fallen on deaf ears. Looking back on that crossing, those were the two most dangerous days I've ever spent afloat.

After the initial carnage, we enjoyed a peaceful crossing except for one incident, somewhere in the middle of the Atlantic, when Locky woke me up around midnight during one of his watches.

'Daz, Daz, sorry to wake you buddy, but I can see a strange light heading towards us,' he whispered as he gently shook me awake.

'What the fuck man?' I exclaimed as I launched myself out of bed and sprinted to the helm. He hadn't been joking, less than a hundred metres away was a little yacht heading on a direct collision course with us. I took immediate action, slamming the wheel over and narrowly missed the boat by twenty-five metres as it sailed across our bow. It continued on, blissfully unaware of how close it had come to calamity, with not a single soul in sight aboard her.

I turned to Locky, 'Jesus H Christ man, we haven't seen a boat on the ocean in over a week and we almost get t-boned by one in the middle of the night. That was way too close for comfort,' I stated more in shock than in anger.

'Well then,' he replied with a sheepish grin, 'it's lucky you got up here quickly then. You're faster than you look, you fat bastard.'

I couldn't help laughing and we spent the rest of Locky's watch entertaining each other with outrageous stories from our past.

There was however a bitter twist in the tail, May. She'd told me in Las Palmas that she had a new boyfriend and I decided to say my goodbyes to her, mid-Atlantic, knowing that she was gone forever. As I sat on the stern of the boat, watching a beautiful sunrise, I took a photograph I still carried of her in my wallet, kissed it, whispered to the wind that I hoped she'd find happiness and dropped it into the ocean. As tears welled up in my eyes, I watched the last of my attachment to her disappear into the distance. A final farewell to the past as I forged my way towards the future I had chosen.

After eighteen days at sea, we rounded Pigeon Island and made our way into Rodney Bay, St Lucia. It was my first taste of the fabled Caribbean Isles and high time to celebrate my first ocean crossing. Locky and I, now as thick as thieves, jumped ship the second we got customs clearance and headed to the first lively looking bar. We ordered beer and rum and proceeded to get well lubricated, tackling each other into the swimming pool whenever the opportunity arose. Throughout the day, our antics got more and more ridiculous until we were finally ushered out of the door after I tackled a local lad into the water. It turned out that he couldn't swim so Locky and I switched from being pro wrestlers to lifeguards and 'saved' the day as we fished him from the pool. As we stumbled back to the boat in high spirits (rum being the main one), we still couldn't work out what would possess a non-swimmer to stand so close to a pool while watching two strangers rugby tackle anyone they could get their hands on into the water. That's just downright irresponsible.

Chapter 5

Christmas in paradise

The party in St Lucia continued for days. We'd made good time for our crossing, finishing in the top quarter of all the boats that entered and every day, more and more yachts rolled into Rodney Bay, bringing with them an endless supply of thirsty sailors to the den of debauchery that is St Lucia. Many a beer was drunk and a tall story told, as my group of friends from Las Palmas swarmed the local bars.

Although Tony and I had our differences, we still got on pretty well and after a few days, he approached me with a job offer. In exchange for covering all my living expenses, my own private cabin and a nominal wage (beer money), Tony wanted me to continue helping him sail and maintain the yacht as he planned to explore the Windward Islands between St Lucia and Grenada with his family and friends for the next couple of months. I was a little reluctant at first, recalling the scarier moments during our Transatlantic crossing, but to sweeten the deal he gave me the use of my own little tender (an inflatable boat with a small outboard motor) so I could be independent and come and go as I pleased when my help wasn't required.

Saint Lucia and its iconic Piton mountains

Even though I didn't have full confidence in his ability as a skipper, Caribbean sailing is some of the best in the world as each island is no more than a day's voyage apart. The sailing risks were minimal, and Tony had offered me the chance to cruise a spectacular part of the world on his floating palace. Getting an opportunity to live the champagne existence on a Coca-Cola income doesn't come around every day so a deal was struck and we set off for Grenada in the south to pick up his wife, Debbie, and their two kids.

Natalie, my book's cover artist, and Lisa making lures

Grenada, although covered in lush primary rainforest, is still a bustling metropolis compared to the smaller, sometimes uninhabited islands that are the true gems in the southern West Indies. After a short stay in Grenada, we made our way back up the island chain to the less populated ones like Carriacou, Union Island, Mayreau and the Tobago Cays. All of the islands are beautiful in their own right, but for me, the Tobago Cays were the most picturesque of the lot. The archipelago is a marine park made up of five uninhabited islands, surrounded by a spectacular coral reef that teems with exotic wildlife. I went free diving every day and never got bored. There were giant starfish the size of dinner plates on the ocean floor and beds of seagrass that attracted a multitude of green turtles who munched away, entirely unfazed by my presence. Photos of the striking white beaches and sparkling turquoise waters were all potential postcards and once ashore, I was startled to find metre long iguanas roaming free, animals tough enough to survive an ocean passage onboard rafts of debris all the way from South America.

I hiked through dry forests of cacti, following a jagged volcanic rock path towards an iridescent sky. On cresting the summit, I witnessed a panoramic view of the surrounding sea as a spectacular sunset lit up the sky and each evening, we'd sit down to a lobster barbecue on the beach, enjoying cold beers from tin ice buckets. I'd sit back, take everything in and be thankful for my good fortune as I joked with Tony, 'Mate, how are we possibly going to survive another tough day in paradise?'

Our island hopping continued through Canouan and onto Mustique, a private island owned by the super-rich, before anchoring in Bequia just in time for the Christmas festivities. Bequia is a stunning little island with a quaint promenade and multihued gingerbread houses dotting the seafront. We'd just arrived ashore to buy some supplies when I was unceremoniously tackled from behind. After regaining my balance, I turned around to be confronted by a beautiful sight. Standing in front of me were the Swedish Vikings, Ludvig, Toby and Simon, who I'd first met in Las Palmas. With their long hair, big beards and bodies covered in tattoos, those pirates were the epitome of mayhem just waiting for a place to happen. I'd not seen those crazy bastards since their last night out in Las Palmas when we'd partied until the sun came up. The next morning, they left to cross the Atlantic, two weeks before I'd set off, in their tiny twenty-seven-foot Albin Vega Sailboat. Their yacht, 'Warskavi af Gamleby' (which roughly translates to 'where are we going?' in Swedish) was so small they removed the toilet to make enough space to store the supplies required to survive the voyage. Tony, always the friendly and generous host, invited the boys back to the catamaran so we could have a proper catch-up. Once aboard the mothership, the Vikings were astounded. Not only did we serve cold gin and tonics with fresh ice from an ice maker (they didn't even have a fridge on their boat), but the Lagoon 560 was wider than their yacht was long and over double the size in length. You could have parked eight Albin Vegas inside Tony's catamaran.

While they were telling me how lucky I was to have sailed the Atlantic in a boat like that, I found myself reflecting and not entirely convinced. They had crossed the ocean enduring the rough conditions and hardship in a 'normal' yacht, pissing over the side of the boat and living off canned food, the way I had always imagined it to be. I knew I was lucky to be living a life of luxury, but in a way, I envied those three sea gypsies.

The reason the boys had sailed to Bequia was to rendezvous with all the other Swedish, Norwegian, Finnish and Danish sailors for the annual Viking Christmas party held there each year.

The Scandinavians celebrate Christmas on the 24th of December which fortuitously happened to be the following day. I was invited to join them for the party, the only non-Viking allowed, which made me feel a little special. We made plans to meet up around noon the next day but not before they wiped out my entire supply of beer.

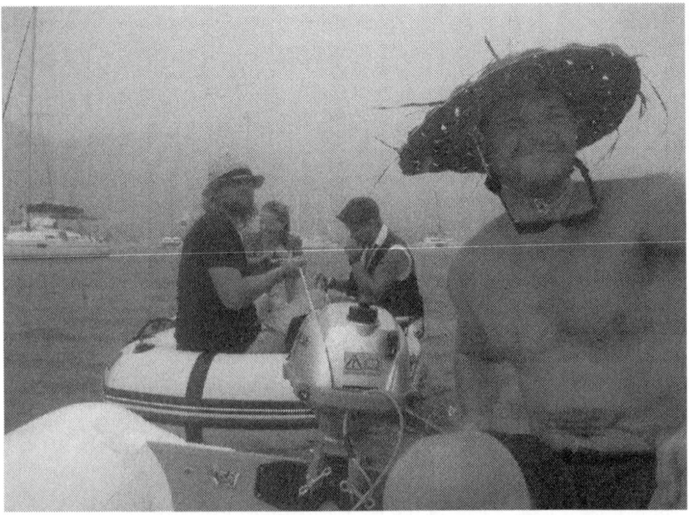

Simon, Johanna, Toby and me getting a little wet

The following day I puttered over to their yacht to find three sweaty men all swearing at their outboard. Their engine was useless and had once again decided to let them down. As much as they laughed at my tiny tender, at least my little outboard had two speeds; slow and stop. So, we rigged a line and I towed them to the beach, all trying our best to look dignified as we bobbed along. That lasted all of five minutes before the heavens opened and we got swamped by torrential rain. No matter, nothing was going to spoil the party as we had plenty of rum and some Swedish sailor's songs to lift our spirits.

Ludvig the Viking and me doing what we do best

We got there in the end and were greeted by a horde of Norseman on the dock. Before I could even disembark my flooded tender, someone had shoved a bottle of Swedish schnapps in my hand, screamed something unintelligible in my ear that sounded distinctly like a war cry and hoisted me onto the quay. When somebody can effortlessly shift eighty kilos of man muscle out of a tender without apparent effort, there's only one thing to say to maintain your dignity.

'Cheers mate! Thanks for the schnapps, can I interest you in a little rum?', I asked, as I waved two bottles of rum in front of the giant human being who had 'rescued' me. Well, that was it, with a big back slap (that almost sent me sprawling straight back into my tender) and a hearty cheer, I was an adopted Viking for the day and proceeded to smash the back end out of Christmas Eve.

Scandinavian Christmas party in Bequia

There were over fifty Scandinavians on the beach that day, hearty people of warrior stock and I loved them all. They seemed to love me too, plying me with exotic alcohol and various selections of preserved fish, a delicacy that tasted way better than its putrid smell.

The festivities continued throughout the day as they always will when you're under palm trees, dancing on an immaculate white beach with a bunch of nutcases, all supplied with an endless amount of alcohol.

I should have followed Toby and Simon's example and slept but by the time I'd located my tender, bailed out all the rainwater and drank a beer I'd found floating in it, I felt like a Viking again and was keen for another mission.

I had an air-conditioned cabin and a king-size bed waiting for me so there was no need for me to deal with the discomfort of pesky mosquitoes and rain showers.

Against my somewhat fuzzy better judgment, I untied the tender from the dock and made my roundabout way home. The water was a little bumpy as gusts of wind whipped through the bay, but I'd dealt with way worse conditions, so I continued on. After getting a little lost and touring through most of the anchorage, I eventually recognised some landmarks and triangulated the boat's position. On arrival, I gave myself a well-deserved cheer for a job well done. Unfortunately, it was rather loud and subsequently woke up Tony's wife. Debbie is a kind soul and she thought she'd offer me a hand to get me on board. I'm sure in any other situation she would have been helpful but, after I handed her the painter (the nautical name for a tender's bow line), she pulled on it just as I went to step onto the catamaran. I lost what little balance I had left, missed the swim platform and plunged straight into the ocean. For the last three months, I'd spent a good third of my time free diving or spearfishing and I'd drunk a fair amount too, so I felt quite at home being a little inebriated in the water and didn't panic. Debbie, on the other hand, started screaming for help and must have only looped the painter over one of the stern cleats in her agitated state.

Tony appeared, understandably not in the best of moods, my manic laughter probably not helping the situation as I treaded water.

'Stop being so bloody stupid, look at the state of my wife, she's freaked out.'

'I'm sorry,' I shouted back.

'Get back on the boat, you idiot.'

It was irrefutable logic and sound advice. I clambered back aboard, apologised for the distress I'd caused, stripped off and fell into bed. I awoke the next morning, naked, bleary-eyed and with a Herculean hangover to the sound of Tony berating me for my irresponsible behaviour.

Five minutes earlier, a local fisherman had returned my errant tender which he'd found floating out to sea. In all the excitement of the night before I'd not checked to see if it was securely fastened to the boat. Tony used my week's wages to buy up the fisherman's supply of lobster and gave what was left of it as a tip for his honesty. I couldn't complain; I'd have been in a world of trouble if the tender had gone missing and I thanked my guardian angels for saving my bacon once again. That Christmas Day we ate a delicious Lobster Thermidor, but for the rest of the week I ate humble pie.

I continued to sail with Tony, his family and friends for another fortnight, but by the time of our third visit to Bequia I'd had enough and decided to jump ship. I'd grown quite attached to Tony's kind and caring family over the time we'd spent sailing together and it was an emotional farewell. Tony gave me a lift ashore and we parted ways over an amicable beer, having a good laugh as we recalled some of our finer moments together. I had enjoyed sailing with Tony, even though most of the knowledge I acquired was more along the lines of what not to do on a yacht. Nevertheless, I had still gained an immense amount of knowledge from the experience and I'd learnt a lot from my own mistakes too.

Once again free, I hit the town that night. I've always loved new beginnings, you get to keep all the positive experiences you've enjoyed, discard all the negative ones and start anew, hopefully, a little wiser than before. I find it exhilarating to embrace the risk of not knowing what's around life's next corner and what amazing opportunities might be waiting for you if you're courageous (or daft enough) to seize the moment. In my experience, if you are willing to confront the unpredictable nature of life with a big smile and a positive outlook, then great things seem to follow.

That evening was no exception. Over dinner, I chatted to an animated chap called Chris, who was passionately watching an NFL American football game on the television. Chris told me over a couple of beers that he'd just landed a job to sail a professional photographer around St Vincent and the Grenadines for the next fortnight. It sounded like an exciting gig, and as I was marooned on the island with no other prospects, I offered my sailing services. Chris mulled it over, decided I was good company and that he could do with the help so the next morning I moved onto his boat, the Dolphin Dancer, and set off once again.

We spent our days scoping out different islands and hotels as the photographer took promotional footage and photos for the tourism board. It was a great week as we took full advantage of the free food and drink laid out by the restaurants as they displayed the best of their menus for the lens.

One afternoon, after yet another free, five-star feed, I was chilling on deck with Chris when into the bay sailed a magnificent superyacht I recognised instantly.

'Raven,' I shouted gleefully.

Raven is a distinctive, all-black Oyster 82, about five million Pounds worth of gleaming beauty and skippered by none other than my mate Andi.

There was nothing for it but to get on the VHF Radio and give him a mighty welcome into the bay.

'Captain Awesome,' I bellowed his nickname down the line, 'it's been a while, compadre. How the hell are you?'

It was wholly against all VHF protocol as the correct etiquette should follow the simple format;

Raven, Raven, Raven. This is sailing vessel Dolphin Dancer, Dolphin Dancer, Dolphin Dancer. Do you copy? Over.

But I was excited and couldn't wait to see my friend again. Without skipping a beat, Andi replied in an authoritative tone, 'channel sixteen is a frequency designated for emergencies and the hailing of other vessels only, stand by on channel sixty-nine.'

He finished the statement with a little chuckle and an almost silent, 'you dickhead.'

I burst out laughing. It was apparent Andi had charter guests on board and when the clients are paying forty thousand US dollars a week to rent the yacht, they expect a professional skipper. He was playing his part to perfection, so I chimed in.

'My apologies sir, I'll be standing by on channel sixty-nine at your earliest convenience. Over'

That afternoon all of Raven's guests were shuttled ashore to catch their private jet home. After weeks of intensive charter work Andi, Hazel (a Scottish lass and the boat's first mate) and Emily (an English girl and the boat's chef), were finally free to let their hair down and relax.

Chris and I were invited onboard to party and we helped the crew get through the last eight bottles of expensive champagne the charter guests had left behind. It was a great night filled with dancing, drinking and midnight swimming and we partied until daybreak. I watched the sunrise from the deck of the multi-million-dollar yacht, as I sipped on the last of the Dom Pérignon in the company of beautiful women and at that moment in time, I knew exactly what it must feel like to be a rock star.

There was a two-week gap before Andi's next charter with a lot of yacht maintenance work to do, so for free board and lodging, I joined his crew and laboured away, getting the boat ship shape for the next set of guests. Our working day fell into an enjoyable routine. We'd all graft our arses off from sunrise to sunset and Andi would be so pleased with how much we accomplished that he'd take us all ashore for dinner. We'd find a party to gate-crash and stumble back to the boat in the early hours of the morning.

We were only expected to work if 'Captain Awesome' was working and Andi resembled a grizzly bear in hibernation when hung over. So, on alternate days we would lounge about the boat, recovering on Bloody Marys and Emily's spectacular cooking. It worked, as long as we were up early the following morning to continue the routine.

One of the many little drinking establishments dotted around the Caribbean

One evening we had just finished cleaning the entire eighty-two-foot teak deck, a large job that had taken all four of us the whole day, when Andi stood up and stated. 'That's it, down tools, we're done for the day. I'm heading ashore in fifteen minutes, so unless you want to swim for your dinner, you had better get a move on.'

Nobody needed to be told twice. After a shower and a quick change of clothes we bundled into the tender and set off. We found a little ramshackle restaurant on the beach and were greeted by Alisha, our convivial hostess for the evening.

After distributing menus, she came back with an ice bucket full of beers and proceeded to take our orders.

'What can I get da ladies for dinner?' She asked in her delightful West Indian lilt.

'We'll have the fish please,' Hazel and Emily responded in unison.

'Sorry, but we gat no fish tonight darlins,' Alisha replied as she turned to Andi to take his order.

'Erm, no fish. I'll try the conch then.'

'My heartfelt commiserations mon, but we don't gat no conch neither.'

She turned to me.

'Goat?' I enquired tentatively.

'Nope, no goat.'

'Well then, what do you have?' Andi asked.

'We gat some chicken,' Alisha affirmed with a massive smile on her face.

'Anything else?'

She shook her head, 'nah, just da chicken.'

Andi looked at the girls and me, then back to Alisha, 'I guess we'll all have chicken then, gorgeous,' he said.

Alisha duly noted the order on her little notepad then slipped it into her pocket. She looked back towards the kitchen area, a small shack.

'Papa, dey all having da chicken,' she hollered back over her shoulder.

From behind the shack, a middle-aged man appeared with a mischievous grin that matched his daughter's as he walked over to another hut. There was a ruffling of feathers, an angry squawk and Papa reappeared with a chicken in his hand, walking back to the shack with a determined strut.

Emily was horrified, 'surely not,' she said.

I shrugged my shoulders. 'I guess so.'

The chicken was squawking again. We all knew what was coming next as its protests ended with the thump of a blade on wood.

Papa's head appeared from behind the shack door. 'No problem mon, dinner be ready in 'bout twenty minutes.'

The chicken was about as fresh as it comes, delicious and made even tastier with crisp, cold beers and an endless supply of local rum. We had so much fun with Alisha over dinner that she invited us out to party with her that night.

The island of Canouan's most famous sportsman, the six-foot-ten NBA basketball star, Adonal Foyle, bought his mother a mansion to live in and she threw a party once a week for the locals. So, off we trooped, driven by Alisha's Papa, to see how much trouble we could get into. On arrival at the villa it turned out that we were the only four white people there and were surrounded by some gigantic, rather intimidating-looking guys. I walked straight up to the largest of the lot, stuck out my hand with a big smile on my face and stated, 'Hi, I'm Daz from South Africa, how's it going?'

That tactic always seems to break the ice and we were welcomed to the party. By midnight we were all suitably hammered and after a great night out, the four of us wobbled into a waiting car and were whisked back to the dock.

'How much do I owe you, my friend?' Andi asked on arrival

The two uniformed men in the front both turned around, shook their heads in wonder and responded, 'are you guys for real? You don't 'ave to pay us, we're da police.'

At the end of the week, Andi dropped me off back in St Lucia as his next set of charter guests were due to arrive. I spent the next two months hitching rides, working on yachts and learning everything I could about sailing. In Antigua, I worked with the renowned skipper, Ross Appleby, on his boat Scarlet Oyster. He had entered the brutal Caribbean 600, one of those 'bucket list' races for all competitive sailors and we got Scarlet ready for the upcoming challenge. Ross will forget more about sailing than I will ever know, and he helped to fill in the gaps in my nautical knowledge over the month I spent assisting him.

A couple of days before the race Ross approached me looking rather solemn. One of his crew had slipped in the shower and broken his ribs.

'Daz, we've got one space left on the boat mate. Would you like to join us for the race?'

I was ecstatic, 'You're joking me.'

'I'm not mate, but it is on one condition. You will have to be the cook for the twelve of us.'

Typically, people pay thousands of dollars to sail with Ross and it was a fantastic opportunity to learn from an incredibly talented sailor. I jumped at the chance, but little did I know it would be four of the toughest days of my life. Even though I got a little respite from the weather three times a day while preparing food, the rest of the time I was on the rail, legs dangling over the water, sleeping where I sat so that Ross could drive the boat harder. For four days I lived in my wet weather gear, sitting up the front of the yacht, taking the full force of whatever nature had to throw at me. On the third night I was rudely awakened while I slept on deck when my lifejacket, soaked for days, finally had enough and exploded into life as the compressed gas cartridge fired. It was definitely not the most pleasant way to be jolted back to reality. By the end of the race, eighty per cent of my body was covered in salt sores and I ached from head to toe, utterly exhausted after only catching snippets of sleep. We won our class though, so all the discomfort and sleep deprivation were a small price to pay for victory.

At the end of March, as planned, Andi sailed into Antigua and I re-joined Raven as part of the delivery crew for the transatlantic sail back to Europe. I'd had a spectacular time in the Caribbean, but it was time for me to head home, sit my Yachtmaster examination, buy a boat and start my big adventure of circumnavigating the globe.

Chapter 6

A love affair

The voyage back across the Atlantic from Antigua, via Las Palmas and onto Gibraltar took a brutal twenty-one days. The 4,000 nautical mile marathon was a constant beat into the prevailing winds. We faced days of relentless storms, raging seas and torrential rainfall. The most powerful squall of them all caught us during the night. It came out of nowhere, spinning our sixty tonnes, eighty-two-foot yacht 180 degrees in a matter of seconds, ripping off the radar unit and damaging the running rigging with winds over sixty-five knots. On the Beaufort wind scale that's classified as hurricane force. Fortunately for all of us, Captain Awesome was on the helm when the squall hit. He took the pressure out of the sails by steering the bow of the boat closer to the wind and his quick reactions saved Raven from sustaining any severe damage. It was another vital reminder never to underestimate the power of the winds that drive our oceans.

On arrival in Gibraltar, it was once again time for Guinness, some fond farewells and a wobbly walk back to the dock. We'd had some great times on both sides of the ocean, both onshore and offshore, and I'd miss sailing with such a great crew.

Raven transatlantic delivery crew:
Ben, Thomas, me, Hazel and Captain Awesome

Once back in England, I had time to reflect on the resounding success of my transatlantic adventure. I'll admit, I was pleased with myself. I'd vastly improved my sailing techniques, my technical know-how and learnt loads of boat maintenance skills. I'd worked out how to deal with people in the cramped confines aboard a boat and found out that I really liked rum! That last one's a bit of a lie, I already knew I liked rum, the Caribbean just confirmed my suspicions. On the emotional side, I'd let go of May. You never know what might happen with the twists and turns of fate, but I knew in my heart that the ocean was my mistress now.

With over 10,000 nautical sailing miles under my belt, I'd gained enough experience over the previous six months to undertake the Royal Yachting Association's Yachtmaster Offshore sailing exam. Mark had already earned his Yachtmaster a couple of years before, so after getting a few pointers from him, I headed down to Portsmouth. After a week's training, plus a full day's practical exam, I passed and legally became a commercial skipper. I hold the Yachtmaster qualification in the same regard as a car driving licence. You go to all the lessons, get cramp from compulsively looking at your mirrors, pass the exam and get a little piece of paper that says you can drive, but you only really learn how to drive after you've got the licence and you're out there on the open roads. The Yachtmaster is no different. The course is excellent and teaches you the necessary skills and manoeuvres required to be safe at sea, but it is no substitute for the hands-on experience that can only be gained by getting out there and getting wet.

While I'd been living it up in the Caribbean, poor old Mark had been freezing his arse off through the British winter and earning his living on his knees. Before you jump to any conclusions, Mark's a tiler by trade, so he's down on the floor on all fours quite regularly. Mark had managed to save more money while I'd been away, but he was still £15,000 short of the forty grand I had in the bank. Nevertheless, we were committed to buying a boat together and Mark had found an absolute beauty situated in Greece.

The previous owners had spent two years renovating their 35-foot Trident Warrior, Hitrapia, Norwegian for 'the little girl of the island of Hitra'.

Their original plan was to sail around the world and they'd outfitted the boat for serious offshore voyages, but after eight years still hadn't left the Mediterranean and decided to call it a day. I guess their dream of long-distance sailing didn't match the gruelling reality of what it's like to spend weeks at sea, getting thrashed about on a little boat.

We flew out to Greece to take a good look at the yacht and the British couple who owned her met us in Preveza. They took us to where Hitrapia was docked and Mark and I fell in love with her immediately. With the classic lines of a traditional Bluewater cruiser, she had a long keel for stability, a self-steering wind vane, autopilot, brand new sails and a ton of other high-end modifications we thought unattainable within our budget. All the original electronics and plumbing had been replaced and the entire boat was almost as good as new with a beautifully handcrafted interior to boot, precisely what we wanted. At £38,000 she was at the limit of what we could afford - we would still need some money left over to live off - but everything else about her was perfect.

After four years of searching, Hitrapia was the one. At midday on Wednesday the 5th of June 2013, we signed some documents, transferred a load of cash and became the proud owners of our very own yacht. After fifteen years of talk, we'd finally put our money where our mouths were and made the start of our dream a reality. With the advent of European summer, I had a sailing instructors' job back in Switzerland and Mark needed to get back on his knees to service the last of his clients so we headed home, happy in the knowledge that we'd be returning soon to start our adventures.

We were both bursting with excitement to get started and the end of summer couldn't have rolled around quick enough. After two months of work and extra cash in the coffers, we prepared to transfer our lives in England to our boat in Greece, but therein lay the problem. Between us we had four kite surfing rigs, kiteboards, surfboards and a bodyboard. We had skateboards, numerous wetsuits, plus assorted spearfishing gear, scuba tanks, fishing rods, reels and all the other necessities required for a life of leisure at sea. Way too much equipment to get on a plane.

Mark, in a moment of genius, decided to buy an old Volvo V40 station wagon in British racing green. It had a month's road tax left on it and cost us a measly £200. V-Bob, as he was affectionately called, trekked across seven countries, numerous language barriers, various service stops and delivered us in one piece to Greece.

Our 2,000 km trip took three days and culminated in a sixteen-hour ferry ride from Ancona in Italy to Igoumenitsa in Greece. In typical style, Mark and I rolled onto the ferry with what we assumed would be enough beer for the trip. It should come as no great surprise that it lasted less than two hours, so we were forced to buy a load of red wine too. This we shared with all our new Greek friends and had a great time. I eventually fell asleep, curled up under an outdoor stairwell on deck six. A blissful breeze and a skin full of alcohol turned out to be the perfect combination to whisk me off for my first decent sleep in days.

V-Bob

The next morning, we made the final short hop from the ferry terminal to Preveza and began the work required on the boat. Hitrapia had been lifted out of the water, placed onshore and sat on a metal cradle with stocks.

All the gear, but neither of us had much of an idea

I couldn't believe it though, even at the end of summer, Greece was still a fierce forty degrees. I was permanently soaked in sweat and to make matters worse, as the temperature dropped in the evenings, squadrons of tiny mosquitos arrived and attacked us like the Luftwaffe. There was no choice but to deal with the conditions as best we could as we laboured away. After a very sweaty and uncomfortable two weeks work in the boatyard, it was time to relaunch her, a daunting procedure that scares even the hardiest of sailing souls.

The afternoon of the launch, a powerful tractor arrived and towed Hitrapia out of her cradle and towards the sea.

When she arrived at the slip, two slings were manoeuvred beneath the boat's hull and attached to a huge crane that loomed above. When they were positioned correctly, one fore and one aft, the crane operator, a bodybuilder who was aptly named Hercules, started to lift Hitrapia skywards. As the boat groaned under enormous pressure, I realised that more than half my total combined assets were dangling precariously in the air and I took a deep breath to calm myself. My heart was pumping and Mark cursed under his breath. The slings looked old and worn and I was acutely aware that they were the only things holding up eight tonnes of my boat as it gently swung in the breeze. It took all of three nail-biting minutes as I watched those slings and prayed that they would hold firm. Hercules manoeuvred the boat over the water, three metres from safety, and slowly but surely dropped her into the drink. Mark punched the air and I gave out a little cheer as we high fived each other before jumping on board to make sure that all the work we'd done was sound. Hitrapia didn't sink and we were both ecstatic. Hallelujah, we'd done it!

I'd won the coin toss (Mark and I solved any mutual decision making by flipping a coin) so it was up to me to pilot the boat on her maiden voyage, all of fifty metres from the slip to the fuel dock. Nevertheless, it was a stressful task, especially on a new boat with various onlookers watching to make sure I wasn't a complete wanker. I managed the manoeuvre admirably - even if I say so myself - and secured the lines just as the spluttering sound of a dying engine kicked in. Shit, we had a problem.

Fuel leaks are marginally better than leaky hulls, but only just. After all the work we'd put in, not to mention the money, it was a heart-breaking moment to see diesel fuel gushing out of the new filter we had just installed. We spent four hours trying to repair it ourselves, but in the end, couldn't work it out and summoned the marina mechanics.

One of them jumped aboard and luckily spoke decent but broken English.

'Not big problem, only little problem.'

'Fantastic, when can you start?'

He looked at his watch. 'Workday over my friend. Tomorrow.'

That wasn't too bad, we'd heard stories about marine mechanics sometimes fully booked with work for several weeks ahead.

I looked at Mark and we both smiled. At least the boat was in the water, what difference would a day or two make?

I slapped him on the shoulder. 'Okay mate, I figure if we aren't sinking it's time to go drinking.'

'Sounds like the perfect plan to me,' he replied.

We arrived at the local taverna and met up with Steve, an old British postman working on his boat in the yard two places down from us. As he'd instigated our farewell committee the day before, we were prepared for the good-natured banter that was sure to follow after only making it to the fuel dock.

'Well done gentlemen,' Steve chided us, 'you almost sailed fifty meters today. By my estimations, it's going to take you just over a million days to make it around the world.'

He placed his hands on his hip and rocked back on his chair as he burst out laughing.

I couldn't let him get away with that as I sat down next to him and shot straight back, 'fortunately we have time on our side, unlike you, you old bastard!'

He cuffed me on the back of the head, 'get the beers in you cheeky little sod.'

The banter continued and centred around the topic of what we were going to do with old V-Bob, our faithful Volvo. We clearly couldn't take him with us but Mark had a plan. He wanted to build a ramp, launch it high into the sky and plunge into the sea like Evel Knievel in a final blaze of glory.

'Are you bloody mad?' I asked.

Mark shook his head, 'no, that's what we are doing, no one is crazy enough to buy it.'

I looked at him and laughed, 'we did.'

Steve the postman

Mark chose to ignore my last comment. I left him and Steve discussing the pros and cons of his approach to asset relocation and I headed to the bar to buy another round of beer, where I found an old lady, perched on a barstool, getting pretty wasted on gin and tonics.

'How are you?' I asked.

'Never been better,' she replied.

It turned out she was English and called Elaine and while I waited for the barman, I chatted to her. She seemed nice enough, albeit a little lonely, so I invited her to join our group. The car debate was still in full swing when we got back to the table. Elaine asked what they were talking about and I explained the story of our 2,000km drive in the Volvo all the way from England.

She took another drink and looked at Mark, 'and you are going to drive it into the sea?'

'Too bloody right,' he replied with a chuckle.

'What a waste,' she said.

And then suddenly I had an idea. 'Elaine, you don't happen to need a car, do you?'

'Well, young man, as it so happens, I need to head back to the U.K. next week and I have mountains of luggage. Putting it onto a plane will cost me a fortune. Does the vehicle run well?' she questioned.

'No issues whatsoever,' I answered honestly, 'it's already made the journey once so there's no reason why it shouldn't do it again.'

'How much do you want for it?'

'How does two hundred- and fifty euros sound?'

'No way,' Mark squealed, 'I'm turning it into a Spitfire.'

'Two hundred and fifty euros,' I repeated to Elaine as she tilted her head and considered my offer.

She placed her glass on the table and stood up, 'show me the car.'

After a quick test drive and a handshake, V-Bob was sold to Elaine for what we bought him for. Although Mark was a little disappointed, in the end, everyone was a winner. Our fuel filter crisis had netted us a great night out, we had drunk lots of beers and had some surplus money from a car that Mark would have only sent to a watery grave.

Hitrapia

Chapter 7

Herby the Hamster

True to their word, the mechanics showed up early the next morning and fixed our fuel problem. After finalising our bill, we waved our final goodbyes to Cleopatra Marina, the mechanics, Hercules and our friends. With some backslapping and high fives we set out to sea, accompanied by the sounds of Stevo's cheers and Elaine honking V-Bob's horn. It was an emotional occasion and I was gripped with a feeling of immense happiness and joy. A wave of euphoria washed over me as I realised the whole world was now my oyster. Mark and I were free to go anywhere we chose, masters of our own ship and our own destiny. I will never forget the overwhelming sense of exhilaration I felt that morning as I contemplated the limitless possibilities that lay ahead.

Where would we go? Who would we meet? What would we see and experience?

I can best describe how I felt that day in terms of a little hamster called Herby. From the first day Herby could walk, he jumped up onto his running wheel in the centre of his cage and set off. In the beginning, Herby quite liked running. All the other hamsters were doing it, so his life seemed fine, it was normal. But as time marched on, all the other hamsters continued their mundane marathon to nowhere, they just kept spinning harder and harder.

This didn't make any sense to Herby. He realised that although the wheel spun faster and faster, he'd been running on the same spot for as long as he could recall. After spending all his energy, he'd not actually moved anywhere at all and it dawned on him that he was only a tiny cog in a giant machine, a machine that had an endless appetite for his energy.

So Herby climbed off from the wheel one day and decided to use his energy for something else. He needed to escape and see more of the world. His cage door was only latched closed, but with a little push it sprung open and he headed off to explore the rest of the big wide world. Herby knew that if he didn't like what he found during his adventures, then the wheel would still be there when he got back as the world continued its inevitable march onwards. There were still millions of other hamsters who would never dream of stopping spinning, consigned by choice or circumstance to their little wheels for the rest of their lives, and that was okay. They were happy with regular food, exercise and plenty of sleep, but Herby wanted a little more and there was nothing wrong with that either.

The day we set sail from Preveza was the day I followed in the illustrious footsteps of Herby the Hamster. I stepped off the hamster's wheel, escaped from my cage and set out in search of a more fulfilling life.

For our maiden voyage, (the short trip to the fuel dock didn't count) we decided to head to the next major island of Cephalonia. Only about thirty-five nautical miles away, it was a perfect distance for a day sail and ideal for us to start getting to grips with our new boat. After successfully sailing through the Lefkada canal and its swinging bridge, in very typical Mediterranean fashion, the wind died halfway through our voyage. With no desire to waste any money on diesel, we decided to spend our first night on anchor and found a beautiful, deserted little bay, surrounded by gently sloping hills covered with olive groves and fir trees.

After all the stress and strain of getting ready to sail, we were enveloped in complete, unbroken, blissful calmness. There was no whisper of wind, no lapping of water, not even the sound of insects. Everything was quiet. After the constant noise of civilisation, the bay was deafening in its silence. This was my Mecca, Medina and Jerusalem all rolled into one. To arrive by sea and embrace the peace and tranquility of nature was as near to heaven as I was ever going to get; it was my holy place. The water rocked me to sleep that night, my soul content, and the last thing I can remember was thinking about Herby's hamster friends.

The next morning, I was up at daybreak and straight into the sea for a session of freediving. If you haven't heard of it, freediving is just about the best thing that has ever been invented. Unlike SCUBA diving, you need minimal–equipment. Just a mask, snorkel and fins will suffice. A decent set of lungs comes in handy too. To start off, all you need to learn is how to oxygenate your blood on the surface and this is achieved by a controlled breathing technique. Once you've 'breathed up,' you take a final maximum inhalation, relax, and then simply dive on a single breath for as long as it feels comfortable. The more you practise, the more your mind and body gets used to the sensation of holding your breath. In essence, you gradually train your body to function with less oxygen and more carbon dioxide in your bloodstream and it's incredible how you progress over time. That morning I could swim down to about ten meters and remain submerged for a minute. Within a few months, I could dive down to thirty metres with a maximum breath hold of four minutes. This may sound like a weird pursuit, to hold your breath underwater for as long as possible, but it's incredibly rewarding and enjoyable once you get into it. When you are freediving the world slows down and you become entirely attuned to your body and the environment. On the surface, you clear your mind and focus all your concentration on breathing. This focus, combined with the feeling of weightlessness you experience once you're submerged, is as close to a meditative state as I've ever been able to achieve. Sitting on the seafloor, wholly relaxed and gently rocking from side to side is one of the sea's greatest gifts. This would become my daily routine whenever we were anchored in clean water, the perfect start to any day.

We arrived in Cephalonia, albeit a day late, to loud cheering from ashore. By one of life's amazing coincidences, Hazel had messaged me the week before to say that Raven would be moored in Fiskado for a couple of days, which made deciding where to go first an easy decision for me. Hazel and Emily walked up the prominent hill overlooking the bay entrance and waved us in. It was a glorious welcome to mark the conclusion of our maiden voyage and a very proud moment for me as I saluted my friends on the ridgeline, pleased that they were there to share this unique occasion with me. Sadly, there was no Captain Awesome as he'd left Raven by that point, but I'm sure he was there in spirit.

Hazel, Mark and me

Hazel kindly offered to swim out and assist us as we anchored and I was glad of the help. Mediterranean mooring is a skill unto itself. First, you drop your anchor, getting it to dig in as you reverse towards the shoreline. Once you're in a position off the coast you're happy with, you swim ashore with fifty-metre ropes and use them to secure the stern of the boat to a tree or rock. Long-keeled boats have a mind of their own when going backwards and the wind was doing its level best to blow us off course while Mark tried to position our yacht into the right spot. It was the first time we'd attempted the manoeuvre and a tough undertaking. On our third try, everything slotted into place as the anchor dug in and Mark made the correct allowance for the wind. I left Hazel in charge of the anchor and sprinted to the stern, looped one end of the long rope around my torso, jumped into the water and swam as fast as I could over razor sharp submerged rocks before clambering up a steep bank and tied the windward line to a tree.

'Take in!' I screamed as Mark pulled in the slack and tied off. I swam back to the boat, repeating the procedure on the other side and that was it, we'd arrived. After giving both Hazel and Mark a big hug (Mark hated hugs, but that was a special moment), the beers were broken out to celebrate.

The first few days in Fiskado were spent with Hazel and Emily, eating, drinking and partying to excess. No big change there. We only had a couple of days together before they headed off on their next charter, so we made the best of it. After they left, I met a beautiful girl named Kate from the Channel Islands. With her dark hair and seductive eyes, she was gorgeous. When you combine beauty with a feisty personality and a wicked sense of humour, then I'm in serious trouble. Suffice it to say, I fell in love with her immediately. Katie was on holiday with her mum Jan, an incredible woman who exuded pure class, the coolest mother and daughter combination I've ever met. We all hung out together and had a ton of fun, laughing our way through the day until my ribs hurt. More excessive eating, drinking and dancing ensued and we had a spectacular week. But like all good things their holiday had to come to an end. We promised to stay in touch and said our fond farewells. This was one of the most challenging things to get used to as a sailor: the endless goodbyes, the forging of fleeting relationships just to see them disappear over the horizon.

Katie

My thoughts always drifted back to Herby and his friends, that wheel and cage. I fully understood why a person could be content enough to stay in one place, in the same job and house until retirement beckoned. Still, no matter how hard I analysed the situation, it was not for me. There's also a positive aspect to this constant flux: it forces you to live in the present, to enjoy and appreciate every moment that you are fortunate enough to spend in the company of good people, fully aware that you may never get the opportunity again.

Mark, Jan, Katie, Kev and me in Fiskado

It was time to get moving as both Mark and I had had enough of the endless partying. We'd both gone sailing to forge a new reality for ourselves and there we were, entangled in the exact same lifestyle of excess that we'd hoped to leave behind us. Enough was enough. It was time to clean up our act and start taking advantage of all the natural wonders that surrounded us. We hatched a plan to head to Mykonos, a kite surfing paradise to the east in the heart of the Aegean Sea. Mark, an accomplished kite surfer, was chomping at the bit to get back on his board. I'd learnt how to kite surf in Morocco about six years before, but I'd done no kiting since and was stoked to get back into some hardcore riding. It was the right time of year to head west if we planned to cross the Atlantic that year, but only buffoons cross an ocean on an untested boat. We still had a whole lot to learn about Hitrapia before then. We may have been two idiots, but we weren't fools.

Before we made it to Mykonos, I hoped to visit a historic site on the Greek Peloponnese peninsula.

'Mate, we should definitely make a stop at a place called Katacolon, it's on the way. It'll be well worth it,' I mentioned to Mark as we sat in the cockpit, planning our route.

'Kat-A-Colon? Did you just make that up or is it some sort of feline rectal dysfunction?' Mark enquired.

He stared at the chart, rubbing a finger along his furrowed brow, 'Ha, I was right, it's a bloody ferry terminal so it's bound to be a shit hole. Looks like a waste of time to me.'

I shook my head, 'A ferry terminal yes, a shit hole most likely, but a waste of time, certainly not. It's the gateway to Ancient Olympia man,' I replied with all the enthusiasm that I could muster.

Mark was laughing loudly now as he dropped the chart onto the table. 'Last time you dragged me out on an archaeology expedition, we found a stone column, a doorway and a donkey. And the donkey looked the oldest of the lot!'

I knew what he was referring to and couldn't argue.

'That's true,' I said, 'but Olympia is the site of one of the major Panhellenic religious sanctuaries of Ancient Greece. It's bound to be more impressive. More importantly, it's the birthplace of the Olympic Games. We've got to go and check it out.'

'Don't forget to take a couple of photos when you get there. You know how much I love to marvel at the sight of an ancient pile of stones in the blistering heat,' he replied sarcastically.

But I was determined to go and used my magical powers of persuasion to talk him into it, which basically translated into bribing him with promises of free-flowing alcohol if he didn't enjoy himself.

He shrugged his shoulders, 'I'll go with that and I'll pay for the beer if it blows me away.'

And so we plotted a course for Katacolon, the arse end of Greece.

On arrival, it turned out that Mark had been right on the money and the port was awful. It is dirty industrial place and we were informed that during the peak season as many as five cruise ships called in there a day.

It was just our luck that the day we arrived was the first time in four months that no cruise ships were scheduled to dock and it was a ghost town. All the residents had taken the day off and headed to the beach. Everywhere was closed; the bars, restaurants, shops and even the local scooter hire place.

Mark was raging, 'how the hell are we gonna get anywhere?'

I was secretly delighted. Ever since his brother had scared him half to death going dangerously fast on his superbike as Mark hung on for dear life, he refused to be the pillion ever again. We'd agreed to rent scooters whenever we went ashore because it was a quarter of the cost of a hiring a car, but Mark left me under no illusions that I would always be the designated bitch on the back. It's bad enough dealing with the emasculating feeling of straddling another man from behind, pottering along on an underpowered scooter, it would have been even worse on this occasion as it was a one-hundred-kilometre round trip to Olympia and I'd have to deal with a broken ass too. In the end we found one car hire outlet open, and as it was the only option available, we splashed out and set off.

Mark

If you ever get the chance to visit Ancient Olympia, then go as it's an unforgettable day of venturing through a lost world. The sprawling archaeological site incorporates over seventy buildings with various temples, altars, statues and numerous other structures scattered around it. Even Mark was impressed as he only expected to see a few scattered stones, and with no cruise ships docking that day, we had the place to ourselves. The amount of architecture still standing was impressive. After strolling through the ruins, we arrived at the Crypt, a thirty-two-metre passageway leading into the Ancient Olympic Stadium. When this passage was first built, it had a vaulted roof, the earliest example of such a tunnel in classical Greece. Even though only the first arch is left standing at the entrance, it is still an incredible feat of engineering considering that it was constructed two and a half thousand years ago. I could just imagine strolling through that tunnel in my toga, feeling the very same excitement I feel today whenever I'm about to watch the fastest men on earth sprint for eternal glory.

Me, doing the Lightning Bolt

I'd wanted to run on the original Olympic track all my life, so I sprinted the two hundred metres barefoot and celebrated at the finish line with Usain Bolt's signature move – the 'Lightning Bolt.'

Our next stop took us to the Olympian Antiquities Museum where I was blown away by the quality and quantity of the artefacts on display. From five-thousand-year-old pottery vases to giant marble sculptures, arts and crafts, military paraphernalia and religious iconography. Just like the archaeological site, it seemed to go on forever and was without a doubt the most significant exhibition of ancient relics I've ever seen, capping off an unforgettable experience. It was a fantastic day and Mark couldn't deny it so much to my delight, the beers were on him that night.

Artefacts in the Olympian Antiquities Museum

After that healthy dose of culture, it was time to take the plunge and set out on a serious passage. We headed southeast out of the Ionian Sea, around the southern cape of the Peloponnese peninsula and turned northeast into the Aegean. It was great to be back to proper sailing again. The cycle of four-hour watches, cooking in a swinging galley and searching for ships' steaming lights in the night felt as natural as breathing. We were back in our element and two very happy chappies. The first couple of days out were pretty uneventful and the only challenge was trying to get back into a sleeping routine on a rolling boat. When sailing offshore, you never know what might be coming your way - bad weather, broken equipment, an illness or an injury, anything can happen. Tired sailors make bad decisions, so it's advisable to sleep whenever you get the chance but during one of my little naps, I was rudely awoken at midday by an incessant recorded message repeating on the VHF.

'Argh,' I moaned at Mark who was on watch in the cockpit, 'what's up with the bloody radio?'

'It's something about warships. It's been going on for about half an hour, but I can't make it out,' he casually replied.

I rubbed my eyes, yawned, stretched and headed to the chart table.

'Warships in Greece, someone's having a laugh.'

After the first few garbled attempts, I managed to decipher the message.

'It seems that there's about to be an imminent naval bombardment of a deserted little island called Karavi, happening between 12.00 and 17.00 hours.'

'BOOM, that sounds exciting, where's Karavi?' Mark enquired.

I perused the charts, marked our position, checked the charts again and started to swear.

'That's Karavi,' I shouted in disbelief, pointing to the island we'd just passed, a few hundred metres away.

'Holy shit!' Mark exclaimed. 'You're kidding me!'

But I wasn't kidding, I was deadly serious and right on cue, the unmistakable silhouettes of seven gunships appeared on the horizon. They were in battle formation and ready to roast our asses for being dumb enough to be anywhere near an island they were about to incinerate.

A frantic VHF conversation ensued as the Hellenic war ships continued their battle formations. After being harangued by the navy's radio operator for about half an hour, we were finally given the all-clear.

'Proceed directly on your current course and speed. Do not deviate or slow down. In accordance with Maritime Law, article number blah states that blah blah blah…' The officer bellowed down the radio set.

'Yeah, great. I'll keep that in mind for the next time we inadvertently stumble onto your navy's shooting range.'

I was having fun now that we'd averted disaster.

'Please confirm that on our current course and speed we will be out of danger by the time you start firing.'

'That is affirmative sir,' came the reply with more than just a little hint of exasperation.

'Do you promise?'

By now they'd run out of patience and a catastrophic sense of humour failure was imminent.

'Proceed with extreme caution. SIR! Hellenic war ships. OUT!'

They couldn't see the funny side of it, but we laughed for ages.

'Hey Mark, what does it take to stop the entire Greek navy?'

'Dunno mate.'

'Just two idiots aboard, abroad.'

Chapter 8

Mykonos Malakas

With the wind on the nose for the final twelve hours of the voyage, we eventually arrived in Mykonos after a tough passage. Sailing becomes disheartening when, for every three miles you travel, zigzagging through the wind, you're lucky if you cover a mile in the right direction. We were both tired but happy to make landfall before dark, heading into the marina just as the sun set. As we made our careful approach alongside the dock, the harbour master appeared, no doubt after his berthing fees. He was shouting something in Greek until he realised we didn't understand him.

'Help?' He questioned.

'We are fine,' I said, 'we're okay...okay!'

Mark executed the perfect manoeuvre and we were gliding in towards the quay in a textbook fashion.

'I don't like the look of him,' Mark said as the harbour master reached for one of our mooring ropes (or warps in sailing jargon).

'No,' I shouted, 'leave the rope, we're okay!'

'We've got it, we are fine!' Mark yelled as he waved his hands in the air.

I looked down in horror as the harbour master grabbed the warp.

'No! No!' I shouted frantically, sensing what was about to happen next.

And it did.

He yanked on the rope, the boat lurched to the starboard side and with a sickening crunch, the bow crashed straight into an unforgiving concrete dock.

'For fuck sake,' I wailed, 'what have you done?'

My patience at that point was exhausted and it took all my self-control not to throttle the fool as I jumped from the boat onto the dockside to inspect the damage.

From the seething look on my face and my white-knuckled fist clenched around a winch handle, he must have sensed his imminent demise.

Mark and I were on our knees, looking at the ding in the hull of our beloved. When we turned around, the harbour master was nowhere in sight, never to be seen again. He didn't even bother to return to collect any berthing fees. The only bonus for his ineptitude was we stayed on and off in that harbour for weeks and never paid a penny.

Thankfully, as we inspected the damage, it was only superficial and wouldn't stop us from sailing. We decided to turn in for the night and reassess the situation in a day or so.

After a much-needed sleep, we walked into Mykonos's charming town centre the following morning. All the houses are built close together - one on top of the other - on narrow winding alleyways, designed that way to enable the townsfolk in bygone days a means of protecting their property from the pesky pirates that ravished their shores. The brigands would get lost in the maze of passageways and be picked off, one by one, from above.

The beautiful white houses of Mykonos

With building materials in scarce supply, the structures are small and functional, yet strikingly beautiful in their simplicity. They are all built in the same orientation to shield inhabitants from the powerful, northerly winds that pummel the island and they have whitewashed walls to reflect the sun's blistering heat. Even the streets' paving stones are bordered in white paint. All the windows, doors and shutters gleam in every pastel shade of blue imaginable and bougainvilleas envelope the blue balconies, their beautiful blossoms providing a colourful contrast to the town's brilliant white interior. With such spectacular architecture, I wandered through a magical labyrinth of twisting alleyways and iconic windmills overlooking the sea, completely enthralled, one of the most beautiful towns I've ever seen.

The picturesque town was a bonus, but we'd sailed there to kitesurf, and I couldn't have designed Mykonos's coastline any better for that purpose if I'd tried. On the south-western tip of the island there are two bays, the mirror image of each other. The first one, Korfos Bay, faces north into the prevailing wind. For kitesurfing you need the wind to blow onshore, otherwise you just get blown out to sea, so the northern bay is perfect for riding.

On the other hand, onshore wind for a yacht is disastrous as the last thing you want is to be blown ashore and shipwrecked. So, it's usually impossible to anchor anywhere near where you want to kitesurf. But therein lies the absolute beauty of this sparkling little isle in the heart of the Aegean. The second bay, Ornos, faces south. It gets offshore wind and that's what you look for when anchoring a yacht. If you're unlucky enough for your anchor to drag, then there is nothing behind you but the relative safety of the open sea. Korfos and Ornos beaches are only separated by a slither of land less than five hundred metres wide; a manageable walk when you're loaded to the gunnels with kiting gear. All in all, a kiteboarding sailor's wet dream.

With those ideal conditions just a short sail away, we left the soulless marina and moved the boat south into a deserted Ornos Bay as soon as the wind settled in from the north. During the peak holiday months of July and August, we were told that more than fifty yachts cram into that little bay and a costly game of bumper boats ensues. We were lucky enough to have the anchorage all to ourselves as it was late in the season. With the northerly Meltemi wind forecast to pump for the next fortnight, we were in for the most epic of Groundhog Days.

Every morning I jumped into the sea, nice and early, to practice my free diving down the anchor chain. Once Mark was awake, we ate whatever was left in the pot from the previous night's cooking, pumped some air into our leaky tender Achilles, piled in with all our kit and headed ashore. We'd chain Achilles to the dock and load each other up with kiting gear. I don't know why we bothered to lock the tender because Achilles' Achilles heel was that he always had a puncture. No matter how many times we tried to fix him, another one mysteriously appeared so nobody in their right mind would have stolen him anyway.

Mark with all our kitesurfing gear in Achilles

Our daily routine was to march the half kilometre between the beaches, waving to the same old lady who swept her veranda every morning and greeting anybody lucky enough to cross our paths with a cheerful, 'Kaliméra.' We were always first to the beach and way ahead of the lazy local kite surfing lads who slept in every day. We'd pump up our kites, attach the lines, don our wetsuits, strap on boards and proceed to kitesurf to our heart's content.

Mark the packhorse

All-day, every day, until exhaustion finally kicked in. This heralded beer o'clock and we'd chill on the beach, raising a can to all those poor hamsters still spinning the wheel in their endless pursuit for more. They could keep their convertible cars, expensive status symbols and all those pointless possessions.

We'd laugh and joke and tell each other how lucky we were and reminisce about another incredible day's riding the wind and the waves in the Aegean Sea. We had a beautiful boat moored up just a few hundred metres away, plenty food and tons of beer. We didn't need anything else. We were happy and loving life - the kings of the world!

We finish each day off the same way, walking along the beach in our flip flops and swimming trunks with a gyros (pita bread filled with thinly sliced lamb, beef or chicken plus salad and a delicious yoghurt sauce) to devour on the way home.

Eat. Sleep. Repeat.

That was our rule of thumb and we never deviated from it. We lived the dream for two phenomenal weeks and it was a tough gig, but somebody had to do it.

Kitesurfing is the sport where you harness yourself to a kite via four or five twenty metre lines. The lines connect the kite to a bar, which you push and pull on to control the kite's flight. The bar, in turn, is attached to your waist harness via a cable which includes an emergency release mechanism to detach you from the kite if it all goes wrong. Once the kite is in flight, you strap a board to your feet, dip the kite to power up and surf across the sea, harnessing the wind to propel yourself at incredible speeds. Once you've learnt how to control the power, it starts to get interesting as you take off, attempting to land tricks after flying through the air. It's a huge adrenaline rush and compulsively addictive. The sky is the limit - if you'll excuse the pun.

Kitesurfing in Korfos Bay

Mark and I were mere amateurs compared to some of the talented riders we met on Korfos Beach. Thanasis, a big, burly, bearded local, could launch himself thirty to forty metres into the air. Looking up at him from sea level, it was as if he was flying higher than the hills that surrounded the bay.

After a couple of days of riding, I asked him how he managed it.

He replied, 'Eh malaka, you just need big balls!'

'Ah, you need to be fearless,' I nodded in understanding.

He smiled, 'No malaka, you just need something soft to land on when you hit the water again.'

Thanasis was the most outspoken of our new kitesurfing acquaintances and nicknamed us dyo malakas, within hours of our arrival.

One day I asked him, 'Hey Thanasis, why do you call us the dyo malakas?'

He frowned and then smiled, 'Because, my friend, it's the perfect description for the two of you.'

Before I could ask any more questions, he was off on his board again.

I later found out that dyo malakas literally translates to the 'two wankers.'

It turns out that in Greek slang, the word malaka can be used as an affectionate term of endearment or as an insult. It can reflect disapproval, awe and admiration or even surprise, depending on the context and manner in which it is expressed. So never call somebody you don't already know a malaka, or you're in trouble. Heaven forbid if you already know the malaka you're talking to and don't sprinkle in a liberal dose of more malakas into every sentence, because if you don't, then that is an insult and you are a malaka!

Mark and I are professional piss takers and soon mastered these new linguistic parameters, using malaka in inventive ways that even had the locals nodding their heads in grudging approval. I always learn the basics of a language like 'please' and 'thank you' for all the countries I visit, but in my wildest dreams I could never have imagined that mastering the local swear words would ever facilitate the easy cross-cultural communication we enjoyed with those magnificent Mykonian malakas.

Alessandro, Tasos, Thanasis and Andreas

Alessandro, Micheal and extrovert Thanasis

Once the guys on the beach got to know us and worked out we were genuine malakas, their generosity was endless. We were invited into their restaurants and bars, hotels and homes. Whenever we tried to pay for anything, they either refused outright, or took our cash and returned with the exact same amount of money in change.

They cooked for us, washed our clothes, organised boat supplies and spares, took us on tours around the island and they even lent us their smaller kites so we could still ride when the winds hit gale force strength. That sort of kindness is unheard of in the world of kite surfing because not only are kites extremely expensive, but they are very fragile if you crash them. Those were just a few of the generous gestures lavished on us during our stay - the beauty of being two sea gypsies. Because we sailed an unpretentious little boat and were quite clearly on a budget, people didn't see us as a cash machine to be exploited when we moored up, but as bona fide travellers to be embraced. We were not a commodity but a curiosity. There was also a definite element of respect and admiration that we had had the balls to leave the hamster's wheel behind.

We met so many kind and hospitable people on the island that it began to feel like our home away from home.

There were also some eccentric folk roaming the island, almost as if a magnet pulled them in, adding a little more spice to the sailing life. Take Bernard, for instance, a softly spoken German in his late sixties who walked up and down the beach playing his saxophone every morning. He lived in a horse box with his dog, a score of stray cats and a multitude of musical instruments, all of which he towed behind his Smart car.

Bernard and his saxophone

An intriguing character, I spent hours listening to his stories of travel and adventure, captivated by his philosophy of complete freedom.

He'd left behind a life of privilege, abandoning his claim as the heir to his family's business and fortune to forge his own path and explore the world. Bernard had built his own trimaran from a sunken steel tugboat and sailed the world's oceans. He'd driven a Land Rover across a continent, starred in a BBC documentary, written books and composed poetry. At fifty, Bernard began to paint, just for fun, after buying a drink that included a free painting set for his young son.

While being interviewed by a German television company about his various exploits, one of the film crew turned out to be an art historian and was fascinated with Bernard's unique painting style. This subsequently launched his painting career and he has exhibited his creations all over the world, selling pieces to some famous celebrities, including Jack Nicholson. But for me, his most outstanding characteristic was how completely content he was with his minimalistic existence in a horsebox, blissfully happy just to live a simple life, camped on a beach, surrounded by his art, his animals and his music.

Then there was Todd the Canadian, Bernard's polar opposite and the only narcoleptic solo sailor I've ever met. Narcolepsy is a neurological disorder that affects the control of sleep. People with narcolepsy experience uncontrollable episodes of shut eye, a ludicrous condition to suffer from if you're a lone sailor. I presume there have been other solo sailors like him, but they haven't survived long enough to make my acquaintance. Todd sailed into the marina and chose to moor next to us, crashing into the dock without any help from the harbour master. He laughed it off, secured his boat and promptly fell asleep for the next twenty-four hours. When he woke up the next afternoon, he told us that staying awake was easy now that his doctor had prescribed him medical-grade amphetamines, it was getting to sleep that was the problem. He'd been awake for three days straight before arriving in port and dinging his boat on the dock, hence his rather prolonged siesta. And bumping into the dock? Well, that didn't even qualify as an accident. The last time he'd fallen asleep while in charge of a vehicle, he rode his motorcycle straight into the back of a truck, regaining consciousness hours later as he lay mangled on the road in a pool of his own blood. A story he corroborated by showing us an impressive set of scars.

'You shouldn't worry,' he said, 'if life has taught me one thing, it's that I am cursed.'

'Really?' I asked.

He grinned, 'yip, cursed to live forever!'

Todd later became rather infamous after replying to a negative comment on his hostel's rating page. He called the complaining lady in question a retard and things escalated from there. Their subsequent spat went viral and made the national news headlines, but Todd survived that too. He may have been a little crude, politically incorrect and opinionated, traits not normally associate with Canadians who say sorry all the time, but we loved his outrageous company and his stories had us in stitches.

Dyo malakas

It was time to bid a fond farewell to Mykonos, our home for the last month. We had kite surfed for the bulk of our time there and when the relentless wind occasionally abated, we chilled with our host of new friends. It was by no means a sad departure as we knew we'd be back to catch up with those malakas again, with plans to return for more kiteboarding as soon as the weather warmed up.

Mark and I decided we'd fly back to England and spend some time with our families over the festive season. If things went to plan, we'd be on the other side of the world this time next year so it may be our last family Christmas for a long time. On our sail towards Athens and the airport, I managed to talk Mark into another cultural day trip to Tinos, Greece's equivalent to Lourdes in France.

Thousands of pilgrims head to this little island every year to pay homage to an icon of the Virgin

Mary, 'Our Lady of Tinos,' one of the patron saints of Greece. As she's reputed to be the protectress of seafarers, I felt it would be rude not to pop in and send her our regards. Mark, who can't abide rudeness of any sort, concurred. The church wasn't difficult to find as we simply followed the long red carpet that snakes its way up the hill.

Panagia Evangelistria and the pilgrims red carpet

As a sign of devotion, pilgrims crawl along on their hands and knees for the eight hundred metres from the ferry pier up the hill to the Panagia Evangelistria church where the statue of the Virgin Mary is housed. Having spent most of his life labouring on his knees, Mark would have found the penance an absolute doddle, but my knees hurt just at the thought of it. Neither of us is religious, so we bought some ice creams and ambled upright towards the summit instead. It wasn't pilgrim season, so we had the place to ourselves. The church is a monastery complex built on the ruins of an ancient religious site and constructed entirely from local marble. It's a magnificent edifice with a beautiful bell tower and the solemn, austere interior of the church is home to the charming 'Chapel of the Apocalypse' where I could just about make out the religious icon of the Virgin Mary in the gloom, covered in votive offerings from devoted pilgrims. To get into the spirit of things I thought I'd light a candle. Although I'm not at all religious, it can't hurt to hedge your bets once in a while.

Our final sailing destination was Aegina, a little island just south of the mainland and a stone's throw away from Athens. Todd, the narcoleptic solo sailor, used a reliable and reasonably priced boatyard there, owned by a guy named Takis Asprakis. We envisaged meeting the Greek version of B.A. Baracus but even though Takis wore less gold and sported a more conventional haircut, he was still our Mr T.

We had some hairy moments as we attempted to squeeze Hitrapia into the narrow slip in powerful winds, but in the end we managed it without damaging anything other than my head when I accidentally head-butted the crane as Takis manoeuvred it into position. Health and safety wasn't too high up on his list of priorities as he popped Hitrapia out the water and swung her ashore with the two of us still aboard. A lot of hammering later, and our little beauty was firmly propped up by a dozen logs and wooden wedges; a basic but effective cradle. Four days of washing, cleaning and preparing the yacht for her three-month winter hibernation followed and we also repaired the damage to the hull from our dock collision in Mykonos.

Mark, showing off on Todd's bike.

Obviously, there's no way on God's green earth that we could clean for four straight days. So, with the help of Todd's illegal moped - it had no brakes or lights - which he left at the boatyard to use on his return, we made regular beer runs to the local shop. After toiling all day, we spent every night drinking and laughing with the two Wims, a Dutch father and son team who were fixing the broken bits on our boat, and Ian, a mad Englishman who did odd jobs around the yard when he wasn't busy building his own yacht.

We were both extremely hungover the morning our flight dawned and for this very eventuality, we'd booked evening flights to allow us more than enough time to make the short hop to the mainland. One thing we hadn't considered though were our travel plans falling on a 'Strike Wednesday.'

Greece was in economic turmoil and the municipal workers, to show their displeasure for the dismal state of the economy, regularly took mid-week breaks, downing tools on a Wednesday. That meant on the only day we needed the civil servants, there were no ferries off the island and no busses to the airport. No problem we thought, a privately-owned water taxi would get us there. But no, there was a severe storm brewing, the sea was in a menacing state and all the water taxis heading north were out of the equation. With all the possible avenues of escape from the island exhausted, we were marooned.

Then our superhero appeared as Mr T strolled over and asked me in broken English, 'what is problem, Daz?'

I explained the situation to him, using a combination of English and my excellent skills in charades.

'Fucking malakas,' he exclaimed.

After pondering the problem for a minute, he tapped me on the shoulder and calmly stated, 'You no worry, my friend. Takis fix.'

With a disregard for his phone bill, Takis called everyone and their dog on the island. After a frantic ninety-minute search, he found an octogenarian skipper willing to dice with death in an attempt to stay ahead of the storm, who transported us directly west to the mainland, 200 km south-west of Athens. He also tracked down his cousin's cousin's cousin, who picked us up from the drop-off point and drove us to the airport, three hours away.

Mr T hadn't finished there. Another of his cousins was scheduled to fly out that evening and Taki strong-armed all concerned, negotiating a bargain price of 300€ in total to be split between the three of us. We got to the airport with about fifteen minutes to spare, a feat of organisation that put Takis firmly in our A-Team. As I sat on the plane and splashed out on a gin and tonic, I was thoroughly content. My first foray into the life of a cruiser had been exceptional and I knew all the sacrifices I'd made to get there were worth it.

Chapter 9

Keep your eye on the prize

Arriving back home helped me to appreciate the amenities that we all take for granted when living in a house. Hot showers, washing machines, satellite television, 240v electric power and a full fridge packed with a delightful assortment of delicious goodies, none of which were available onboard. On Hitrapia we had a two hundred litre water tank that lasted the two of us almost a month. To put it in perspective, that's the equivalent amount of water used in three average showers or two loads of washing. Living on a little boat teaches you how to conserve your resources and it felt wrong to waste water unnecessarily so I still only took short showers, but in a tiled bathroom with hot water it was pure paradise.

We'd planned to be back in the UK to work for three months and earn more travel tokens to subsidise our adventure. After a week of lounging about, meeting up with friends, family and generally taking it easy, it was time for me to face the harsh reality of finding a job. I approached a few agencies and signed up. Within thirty-six hours, they found work that suited me perfectly - their words, not mine - and I landed a job in a crisp factory.

Mine, al mine!

Here is a short account of the misery that followed. My alarm clock would wake me at 4:00 am for a 5.30 am start every morning. I'd gobble down a quick breakfast and set off on the one hour walk to the industrial estate in the freezing cold, wet and wintery gloom. On arrival, I signed in at three different locations and collected my protective clothing for the day which consisted of a red hairnet, earplugs and a disposable white overall. The sexy ensemble was completed with steel toe cap boots, a safety helmet and a snood to cover my facial hair. I'd wade my way through a sea of discontent as the permanent workers lined up to clock in for their shift. Nobody mustered a smile, they all looked like condemned men heading to the gallows. After sanitising my hands, I made my way to a little square reserved for agency staff. The shift manager guided me to a conveyer belt, gave terse instructions and for eight hours a day I was on the production line, packing snacks into boxes as a 'crisp relocation engineer,' the lofty title I gave myself in one of my more inspired moments of utter boredom. Every two hours I got a twenty-minute break, which I thought was a generous gesture from Tayto's directors, until I found out that all breaks were unpaid. This delightful way to spend my day netted me the grand total of £6.31 per hour - national minimum wage - and not even enough to buy two pints at the pub.

The work wasn't taxing and only required minimum dexterity, but it was the repetition that almost drove me insane. The hardest thing of all was looking around the factory at a scene from the Living Dead. My fellow workers resembled automated zombies, emotionless and sallow shadows of human beings. One of the workers I chatted to over my unpaid lunch break, Derek, had been working on the same production line for twenty years and I couldn't help but feel sorry for him as I imagined waking up every day to a life of such monotony, knowing it was my fate for the rest of my life. At forty-five years of age, Derek had no ambition to improve his lot and he still had another twenty years to go before retirement. He'd have got less time in prison for murder.

Seeing all those human hamsters just made me realise, once again, how fortunate I was to be embarking on my incredible adventure of sailing around the world. I knew I was lucky; in different circumstances, I too could have been a Derek, with no option but to slave away in a similar situation just to make ends meet. I think life is like a game of poker, you just have to play the best you can with the hand you're dealt, but as my mum likes to say, 'you might be lucky, my boy, but you make your own luck too.'

Christmas came and went. It was great spending time with my family, but I missed the ocean. I missed waking up to the fresh and intoxicating smell of the sea and the excitement of not knowing what was going to happen next. I missed meeting new, interesting people and exploring unique places every day. In a nutshell, I missed being free.

'I'm not sure how much more of this I can take,' I said to Mark over a beer at his local pub, huddled near the fire in the depths of a freezing British February. I'd secured myself a better agency job in another crisp factory, but it was still purgatory.

'Me neither mate, I've got a month of tiling left in me then we've got to bounce.'

We both agreed and booked flights back to Athens at the beginning of March. With a light at the end of the tunnel, my last few weeks as a snack packing professional were bearable. The only times in my life when I've ever felt trapped, or in a rut, always occurred when I had nothing to look forward to. It's vitally important for your sanity to work towards a goal, however big or small that goal may be. Keep your eye on the prize, stay focused, and anything is possible... even packing crisps for future travel tokens.

The flight back to Greece was an adventure in itself. Our time aboard Hitrapia had shown us what we were lacking for the rest of the voyage and we procured all the necessary equipment needed. I'd bought three new kites and a compact manual clothes washing machine to name but a few items. With a pack on both my front and back, plus a hold-all in my left and right hands, I was carrying a staggering eighty kilograms of luggage. Mark had about half that weight, but his luggage included our new outboard motor, a massive, cumbersome crate to carry. It was a tough haul, but now we had everything we needed for our circumnavigation.

Back at the boatyard, the Wims had rebuilt all the broken things we were unable to fix ourselves. Wim Senior had even gone to the trouble of putting together an emergency fibreglass repair kit as a leaving present for us. The world's oceans are littered with shipping containers that have fallen off transport ships during transit and they can easily puncture a fibreglass hull if you hit them, so his gift was gratefully received. Owning your own yacht is a very steep learning curve. We'd already learnt a considerable amount about our boat, but Mark and I both wished that we could have shrunk down the two Wims to pocket size and taken all their skill and knowledge with us on our journey.

We were all set to leave so I booked a launch time for the next morning. With nothing left to do but risk life and limb on Todd's moped, we popped to the shop and bought their entire stock of beer for our leaving party. Things quickly deteriorated into drunken debauchery and the night was going great guns until Insane Ian dared Mark to eat the entire contents of a pepper shaker.

Now here I need to explain why Mark is not your run of the mill kind of an idiot, but in a special class of his own. For his first tattoo, Mark had his entire back covered in over eighty hours of inking. He decided he didn't like it and underwent weeks of laser therapy to remove it - which according to him is twice as painful as the initial tattooing – then had his whole back tattooed a second time. So, a disregard for pain, a susceptibility to dares and alcohol-fuelled bad judgment are just a few of the characteristics that make him 'special.' Don't get me wrong, I can be an idiot too.

I'd recently lost a dare to Mark and he injected me with an out of date EpiPen (an epinephrine auto-injector I use to counteract anaphylactic shock brought on by my allergy to bee stings). It resulted in a massive bruise down my leg and a knee that wouldn't bend for three days, so I suffer from the same affliction of general silliness, albeit to a lesser degree. But Mark, with Ian egging him on, proceeded to chug around fifty grams of pepper in one sitting. It was one of the dumbest things I'd ever seen him do, and trust me, the list of stupid things he's done is a long one. He managed it, although he did look a little red in the cheeks. After washing it down with a beer he stated, 'Too easy, that was a piece of piss!'

Mark woke up the next morning as sick as a dog so I spent my day reading a book in the cockpit, laughing at him every time he appeared from below to spew over the side. It delayed our departure by a day but made no difference in the grand scheme of things as we weren't in a huge rush to get anywhere. He felt human again after flushing himself out for twenty-four hours and we repeated our fond farewells to all the great characters that made up Takis Asprakis's boatyard before launching on of our next adventure.

A sporadic wind forced us to moor in Aegina harbour for a couple of days before we could make the short trip south to Poros. It was high time for Round Two of mission Mykonos as we missed our malakas and both had new kites to play with. So, at the first sign of a decent day's wind from the north, we made the overnight voyage back to our beloved isle and anchored up in the familiar bosom of Ornos Bay.

After a quick sleep, we hit the beach, but it was a disappointing day. The wind was too gusty for us to kite safely and unpredictable wind became the hallmark of a frustrating three weeks stay. Such is life. If conditions were perfect all the time, then there'd be nothing to look forward to.

We still had some great days though. During one of those good sessions we bumped into Anna, a half Russian, half Greek girl who we'd met on our last visit to Mykonos. I'd spoken to her a couple of times before, but she'd obviously taken a shine to Mark and I noticed numerous attempts on her behalf to strike up a conversation with him, but he blanked her every time. Mark wasn't playing hard to get; he just couldn't seem to read the signals that were so obvious and it was painful to watch. This day was different though as she managed to ambush him while he was packing away his kite. After some chit chat Anna invited him, and by extension me, to go out clubbing with her that evening. With waist-long curly dark hair, a gorgeous smile and a super model's body squeezed into a revealing wet suit, I'd have walked over and slapped him on the spot if he'd said no to her. He managed to nod a yes and she arranged to pick us up at midnight. We thought it was a ridiculous time to start the night's festivities, so in the true British tradition, we began drinking as soon as the sun went down and by the time Anna picked us up five hours later, we were ticking along nicely.

‘How did you guys meet?’ Anna asked us once we'd arrived at the bar.

‘Through mutual friends,’ I replied.

‘And how long have you been together?’

‘We bought the boat about a year ago,’ I replied.

Alarm bells started to go off in my head. No, she couldn't possibly be thinking…

‘You must have known each other for years to make that kind of commitment to each other,’ she stated as she twirled her cocktail straw.

‘Erm, yeah,’ I said, ‘we've been planning to make this trip for over a decade.’

I could see where this was going, but Mark was completely oblivious as he stared into her eyes.

Anna took a drink and placed her glass on the table. ‘It's so beautiful to meet a couple brave enough to follow their dreams together.’

At last Mark finally clicked what was going on and spluttered his beer all over the bar. I couldn't help but burst out laughing. This was typical of Mark's luck; the first girl to show any interest in him on the trip and she put two and two together and decided he was homosexual.

‘That's fucking priceless mate,’ I managed to say with tears rolling down my cheeks. I could hardly breathe, ‘Sorry, I better stop calling you mate, people might get the wrong idea.’

Anna's look of disappointment disappeared, ‘I don't understand. Aren't you gay?’ she said, staring at Mark.

‘Jesus, if I were gay, I'd have much better taste in men than that ugly bastard,’ he stated, pointing at me.

This was manna from heaven; a new stockpile of future ammunition to aid in our perpetual war of wit as I pursued my relentless quest of taking the mickey out of Mark.

Once Mark had ironed out that little misconception and I'd recovered from almost wetting myself, Anna explained that Mykonos has a sizable gay community and apologised for her assumption.

'Don't worry about it, we get it all the time,' I lied to reassure her and continued to blow kisses to my tubby 'husband' for the rest of the night. It turned out to be a great ice breaker though as we all laughed about it and she was relieved we weren't offended.

Mark is actually quite a handsome chap who looks a bit like Robert Downey Jr with Jack Nicholson's smile. Now that Anna realised he was single, she was into him, flirting suggestively. I was rapidly becoming a third wheel and beat a hasty retreat, chatting to some of the malakas from the beach

At one point, Anna nipped to the ladies' room and Mark wandered over.

'Daz, I'm not sure, but I think Anna might like me.'

I shook my head in consternation.

'Of course she likes you, Dickhead. That's what all the hair twirling and body contact's about.'

'Yeah?'

'Yes. All you have to do is play it cool for a couple of hours, then ask her to take you home.'

He grinned. 'All right, I'm on it like a gin and tonic,' he stated with a newfound air of confidence.

'Oh, I bet you are. You've got this boy,' I replied, knowing full well that he didn't.

'Just remember Tropic Thunder, mate (Mark's favourite movie). Never go full retard,' I shouted to his retreating back. I hoped against hope that it might have the implied effect. All he had to do was hold it together for a couple of hours - not a mammoth task, one would think.

He started off well and after thirty minutes, he hadn't done anything too ridiculous. I gave him the thumbs up, silently mouthing, 'ninety minutes to go bro, you're doing well,' to which he responded with one of his big, goofy smiles, but his self-control didn't last long.

Anna, Andrea, me and Mark all ready to party

'Sorry dude, I just can't help it, it's time for a bad dance-off,' he cried ten minutes later, starting to bust out his favourite granddaddy dance moves in front of me. When dancing, Mark looks like he's having a seizure, but it's done with such delight it's impossible not to get swept away by the absolute absurdity of it all and have a wicked time joining him. To my great surprise, Anna hustled in next to us and started to throw down some ridiculous shapes of her own. She loved the silliness and Mark had met his match.

On the stroke of 3am, Anna decided that it was time to head home, jingled her keys in front of Mark and said, 'let's go.'

I was about to break out in spontaneous applause when, to my astonishment, I heard Mark say, 'Na, I'm staying here. I wanna dance baby.'

As her face dropped and my soul cried out for some sanity, Mark spun on his heel and started to do some sort of Harlem shake. Anna, in complete disbelief, shook her head, gave me a hug and headed home... alone. If Mark wasn't the biggest idiot on the planet, then he was definitely on the podium. But one thing was for sure, there was never a dull moment in his company and I was lucky to have him along for the ride.

Chapter 10

Karma storm

Mark never managed to hook up with the beautiful Anna although he did try and woo her over the next week, but in the end, he ran out of time. We were scheduled to pick up his parents down in Crete to take them on a ten-day sailing holiday and, unlike the last parting from our Mykonian malakas, this time was a sad occasion because we didn't plan on returning. We'd already spent over two months with those dudes and they'd adopted us as two of their own. Their kindness and generosity had been limitless and I hoped one day to be in a position to repay the favour, even if it's a simple case of paying it forward to some other sailors who wash up on my shore in the future. If only everybody in the world were so willing to give more than they took, then we'd live in a paradise on earth.

The sail down to Crete wasn't sailing at all. With no wind we motored for fifteen hours, something we wouldn't normally do as every litre of fuel the boat drank was a dent in our beer kitty, but we had no option. Mark's folks were flying in and we had a deadline to meet.

Mark with his parents, Lynn and Laurie

We docked on Chania's town quay, gave the boat a spring clean and changed the sleeping quarters around. I moved from the bow to the stern cabin to make way for Lynn and Laurie, Mark transferred into the saloon. It was a lucky move on my part as Laurie's snoring can wake the dead and Mark didn't sleep for days. Like all good mothers the world over, once onboard Lynn vastly improved the menu by including loads of healthy salads and fruit with every meal, a welcome change from our staple diet of beans, lentils and root vegetables. Laurie busied himself pottering around the boat, fixing everything, even the things that weren't broken until he started fiddling with them.

We rented a car to explore the north of the island and visited Elafonosi's famous pink beach. Created from tidal deposits of pigmented microorganisms that live symbiotically with the local seaweed, it's a majestic contrast to the pristine turquoise waters lapping its shore.

Graffiti in Crete

Another tough day swinging in my hammock with the snow-capped mountains of Crete in the background

We drove through the mountains and investigated an underground cave system and Mark's parents even spoilt us with restaurant meals, something we rarely enjoyed. Living on such a limited budget had its drawbacks, but it did make us appreciate the finer things in life when we got the chance. Our nights were whiled away over a bottle of wine or two, enjoying each other's company in complete tranquility. After a week of anchoring in yet another beautiful bay, Lynn and Laurie began to understand why their son decided to chuck in the life of a labourer and instead embrace the cruising lifestyle.

After their departure, it was time for pastures new. We'd spent six months exploring the Greek Isles and as good as it was, the world's an enormous place and there was plenty more to explore. Situated 450 nautical miles directly west from Crete is Malta, a little island with a big history. Due to its strategic location right in the middle of the Med, Malta has been an important naval base for millennia and permanently inhabited for almost eight thousand years. Ruled by a succession of powerful nations from the Phoenicians to the French and every other major naval power in between, the island is steeped in history. With all those various influences, the island is scattered with archaeological sites including seven megalithic temples, some of which are the oldest free-standing structures left on earth and I was eager to go exploring.

We waved goodbye to all the tourists walking the dock in Chania and made our way out to sea. With steady winds and little swell, it was the perfect start to our first, long voyage. Nothing untoward occurred until a day into the trip when we had a surprise visit from a little lost swift. During big storms, birds are often blown off course and the little guy was a long way from home. Swifts spend most of their lives on the wing, seldom needing to rest, and it was the first time I ever saw one circling a yacht. I called him

Swifty Steve. He was somewhat weary of us to start with, but within a few hours his fatigue eclipsed his fear and he landed on our solar panel, exhausted, but after a little siesta he once again took to the skies. The nearest coastline was sixty miles away and we hoped he'd make it as he disappeared over the horizon. We'd grown quite fond of Steve so imagine our surprise and delight when just before nightfall we spotted him circling the boat again. After a couple of test flights inside the saloon, he found a spot he liked and made himself at home. Within a few hours, he was perching on Mark's shoulder as he cooked or on my head as I read.

Swifty Steve

Swifty must have been in dire straits to seek haven with us humans, but as far as we were concerned, he was welcome to stay as long as he liked.

For the next day, Hitrapia was Steve's home too. He was a little character and shat on my head twice, so I figured he had a decent sense of humour.

He didn't overstay his welcome though, as I woke the next morning to the sad news from Mark that he'd died during the night. It was such a shame, if he'd only been able to hang on for another two days, we'd have safely delivered him to Malta where I could have caught some insects to help him get his strength back. We consoled ourselves with the thought that at least he spent his last day chilling on Hitrapia in the company of friends, instead of flying until he pitched into the water from sheer exhaustion. We decided to bury him at sea and before we consigned him to the deep, I had a few kind words to say to mark his passing from this world:

There once was a swift called Steve.
Who needed a lift, I believe?
He was too tired to fly,
and sadly, he died.
So now all that he gets is a heave.

Other than that sad little interlude, everything was superb. We worked out how to set up the self-steering wind vane, Manny the Monitor, a genius mechanical invention that uses small changes in the wind direction to bring the yacht back on course. Once the boat's sail configuration was balanced and Manny was set up correctly, he only required the occasional tweak, but otherwise steered the yacht better than a human. The best thing about Manny was that he never got tired, never complained and we didn't have to feed him.

Thanks to him, it was hands-free sailing. With no helming to do, cruising on a sailboat is idyllic, freeing up time for the essential things in life like relaxing in the sun with a good book, a slab of chocolate and an ice-cold beer. The only thing left to do was scan the horizon every ten minutes on the lookout for other vessels, but that wasn't too taxing. I simply swivelled on the spot and surveyed my majestic three-hundred-and-sixty-degree panoramic sea view for ten seconds. Job done and just another tough day at the office.

After a few days sailing, we arrived in Malta's main port of Valletta and it was rammed. Every single marina was full and all the mooring buoys were taken. There wasn't a free spot big enough to swing a cat in. When I'd done my research, I hadn't paid attention to the fact that Malta is one of the smallest, yet most densely populated countries in the world, and space is at a premium. After an hour's search, we found a gap just big enough for us to squeeze into on the yacht club's pontoon and I jumped ashore to find out how much it cost per night. Mark and I were each living off a budget of 250 euros a month, which was plenty of money as we typically anchored for free. After a quick reconnaissance and a chat with an Aussie lad polishing a powerboat, I headed back.

'Well, there's good news and there's bad news bud,' I reported to Mark, 'the bad news being that there is no good news.'

Mark shrugged his shoulders and frowned, 'Shit, what's the damage then?'

'The Aussie lad reckons everywhere around here is full and this is the cheapest spot we're likely to find. It'll be anywhere upwards of 60 euros a night.'

'You must be joking' he replied, 'we've spent less than a hundred euros on moorings for six months in Greece. Sixty a night is daylight robbery!'

Mark was spot on. I pondered our delicate situation, looking around to see if anyone official was heading our way.

'I have a plan,' I said.

'Yeah?' Mark questioned.

'They can only make us pay if they catch us,' I pointed out with a wink. 'I've been cooped up for too long and I'm hungry and thirsty so let's explore the town.'

Mark stated the obvious, 'They'll be waiting for us when we get back.'

I shook my head, 'Not if we go on a bar crawl and come back so late that they'll all be tucked up in bed.'

'Sounds like a plan,' Mark said.

So, we snuck out of the yacht club and hit the town.

We found a local supermarket and resupplied with fresh fruit, vegetables, water and beer, our essentials for survival at sea and returned to the dock at midnight when the bar closed. Everything went to plan as we staggered back to Hitrapia without seeing a soul. We beat a hasty retreat at first light, making it back to sea before anybody collared us for cash, deciding that as lovely as it was, Malta was way too expensive for these two sea gypsies.

The world works in mysterious ways and we were soon reminded why honesty is the best policy. Within a day of leaving Malta, we sailed straight into a gale which hadn't been forecast. I nicknamed her Karma-gale and she proceeded to slap us down for skipping town without paying our dues. With wind gusts over forty-five knots and steep, breaking seas, things started to get pretty gnarly. The waves came from all directions and we were repeatedly drenched, standing in water up to our knees as the cockpit drains struggled to deal with all the water washing in. While I helmed at the height of the storm, we barely escaped two knockdowns as rogue waves battered our beam, forcing the boat over on her side and pushing the top of the mast to within metres of the turbulent sea. The yacht heeled to sixty degrees each time it happened, and it felt as if it were about to fall off the edge of the world, but Hitrapia was designed with a long, heavy keel for that very reason and she self-righted herself. It was tough on the two of us as we beat into the storm for forty-eight hours and only made a paltry forty miles of headway. With conditions far too severe for Manny to operate, we had to hand steer day and night. To facilitate this relentless helming, we changed our watch rotation to two hours on, two hours off. The unpredictable waves meant total concentration at all times and at the end of each watch, I stripped off my wet weather gear and crawled into my sleeping bag in the saloon berth Mark had just vacated, the only place on the boat that didn't feel like you were on a rollercoaster. I'd strap myself in with a lee cloth to prevent getting flung across the boat and wedge in as many pillows as I could to stop myself rolling around. With the wind howling and waves crashing against the hull, I'd try to get some sleep but it was like being in the bowels of a giant washing machine without the soap and flowery fragrances that would have made it more bearable.

After the first twenty-four hours I was so tired I'd simply flop onto the saloon floor, wet weather gear and all, curl up and pass out until what only seemed like minutes later, Mark would wake me up for my next two-hour shift. Karma-gale was tough on the boat too. We snapped the foresail furling line, cracked the cooking gas regulator and a washboard (a wooden slat that acts as a door to secure the passageway from the cockpit to the saloon) was dislodged and lost overboard. No longer capable of ensuring the watertight integrity of the yacht and unable to cook any food, we were forced to head for the closest safe haven and hide. Battered, bruised and looking rather bedraggled, we scampered into the port of Isola di Marettimo, west of Sicily, anchoring in the harbour at midnight and making our way to the small pier at first light.

It was our first proper storm aboard Hitrapia and she'd sailed through with flying colours despite a few minor mishaps. We were now convinced that she was tough enough to sail around the world and we'd begun to learn how to cope with severe weather conditions on our boat.

Marettimo has a tiny harbour and the dock only had space for three boats. We managed to squeeze into the last available spot, ecstatic to tie up to something solid and stop the continuous rolling we'd endured for days. As other weary yachtsmen limped into port, they were forced to raft alongside us, beam to beam. We got parked in by two old German sailors, Peter and Herbert. They were pushing seventy and had clearly taken a pounding from the storm, both looking utterly exhausted and not far from death's door. Mark and I were both young, fit and robust and that storm was a gruelling test of our stamina, so I couldn't imagine how knackered those old seamen felt. Our new neighbours went straight to bed and we didn't see them again until the next morning after we all had a good night's sleep.

When we woke, the storm had abated and the wind had switched back to a favourable direction. We located a spare gas regulator in the port's little fishing village so it was time for us to head back to sea, but Peter and Herbert had different ideas. They didn't trust their engine and one excuse followed another until, hours later, Mark and I gave up trying to get them to let us out. We couldn't force them to move and any more stress may have killed them. In reparation for the inconvenience of parking us in, Peter and Herbert thought it was only fair to invite us over to get hammered on their stock of beer. We happily obliged and drank their boat dry, confirming the fact that Germans, whatever their age, can drink with the best of them.

The enforced layover allowed me to head out at 5 am the next morning to explore the island.

Isola di Marettimo

Marettimo is the most westerly isle off the coast of Sicily and its remoteness has been its saviour; there are no cars, only one hotel and very few tourists. I hiked the nature trail to the lighthouse on a delightful coastal path and didn't see another soul all morning. I did see a lot of wild goats, horses and donkeys and a magnificent sunrise as the sun illuminated the retreating storm clouds from below. Invigorated after my walk, I returned to the dock to see a group of decrepit old locals, faces lined and worn from a lifetime at sea, all armed with walking sticks and almost bent over double from the ravishes of time, all having a heated debate as they gesticulated at each other and pointed towards Hitrapia. They made Peter and Herbert look like proverbial spring chickens and I reappraised my concept of what constituted old. It soon became apparent what the problem was as this gaggle of toothless wonders communicated their discontent.

In sailing, it is customary to fly the national flag of the country you visit just underneath the spreader on the starboard side of your yacht. It's called a courtesy flag and is seen as a mark of respect. In our rush through Malta and our exhaustion post-Karma-gale, we'd forgotten about the courtesy flag and still had the Greek one fluttering in the wind. It was clear that they weren't too happy with our oversight. I shouted to Mark who grabbed the Italian flag and rapidly hoisted it before we had a riot on our hands. Technically we should have raised the yellow quarantine flag as we hadn't been cleared by customs to enter the country, but desperate times require desperate measures.

As Mark lowered the blue and white striped Greek flag, a huge cheer erupted. Then, as he started to hoist 'il Tricolore' (the Italian flag, we didn't have the Sicilian one), all the old boys on the dock removed their hats, placed their right hands on their hearts and belted out the Italian National Anthem. It was a beautiful sight; they sang in tune with perfect harmony and the hairs stood up on the back of my neck. I looked at Mark as a smile pulled across his face. The four old geezers with rheumy eyes shed a tear for their beloved country and it wouldn't have surprised me if some of them had served in the Second World War. With their patriotic duty for the day concluded they were now all smiles and after pouring us each a shot from their communal bottle of alcohol (that could have doubled as paint stripper), they saluted us and toddled off to drink away the rest of their day.

With conditions calm and Peter and Herbert well-rested, they were happy to shift their boat and we headed out. Even though it had only been a whistle-stop stay on Sicilian soil, Marettimo was a magical little island and I shall always remember it as the place to go if you want to get pissed with pensioners.

Local fisherman selling their catch

Chapter 11

Picking up the pieces of a shattered dream

It was still a long way to the Atlantic Ocean, so we spent the next three weeks heading west. We bounced from Sicily to Sardinia, onto Menorca and finally dropped anchor in the large, well-protected bay of Alcudia in the northeast of Mallorca. Mark had a couple of friends on the island who he'd met kitesurfing in Thailand. One was Ronny, a German marine engineer and the other was Lewis, an English ice-cream vendor who were both generous to a fault. It was great to have local knowledge and a ready-made crew to ride with on Pollensa Bay, Mallorca's enormous kiting beach on the west coast. It stretches for over six kilometres with shallow water and powerful winds, a kite surfer's paradise. Unfortunately, it was forty kilometres from the anchorage, so we only headed over there when the wind was pumping and somebody was kind enough to offer us a lift.

Before we could have too much fun though, there was a long list of boat jobs to sort out; work we had put off for too long. The biggest was to replace the washboard lost in the storm off Malta. I didn't have the tools required to construct the replacement, but as luck would have it, Ronny had an entire workshop equipped with all the tools I could imagine like jigsaws, routers, circular saws, electric sanders and drills. You name it, he had it. A job that would have taken me a week to complete without power tools was finished in a day. Ronny also knew where to get hold of all the spares Mark and I needed to complete the myriad of other tasks on our to-do list. He was a lifesaver and you'd struggle to find a more genuine, helpful and thoughtful character and as two kindred spirits, we took to each other immediately.

Throughout the day, we shared our thoughts on life, love and our mutual appreciation of music as we worked on various projects, helping each other out whenever necessary and quickly building a camaraderie based on mutual respect and competence.

Once my jobs were completed, I was free to head back to the boat and kick back for the day. After weeks of night watches and broken sleep, it was great to be on anchor again, getting lots of rest and making loads of new friends. Alcudia Bay was full of a range of interesting cruising sailors and I got to know them all.

Yves and his wife were a charming French couple in their sixties who sailed a similar boat to ours. They had lived a simple lifestyle aboard for over thirty years. Yves was always inviting me over for a game of chess and a bottle of red wine. We'd communicate with each other in pidgin French or English and take turns to cook each other dinner.

There was also Marc the Belgian, who spoke five languages fluently and sailed with his wife. He had sold his beer exporting company and lived on a brand new, sixty-foot superyacht. We drank imported craft beers together (of which he seemed to have a never-ending supply), as we watched international football matches, streamed aboard via Dutch satellite television while Marc cooked Argentinian steaks on his barbecue.

Belgian Marc

Yves and Marc were from the two opposite ends of the cruising sailor spectrum, but that was the beauty of my new life. When you immerse yourself in the cruising lifestyle, you get to meet the most amazing people from every walk of life. I enjoyed spending time with these disparate characters so much that I would often spend days without setting foot on land.

Mark was nowhere to be seen though. He'd managed to get a liveaboard job on a tourist boat, skippered by another sailing friend of his and disappeared for two weeks.

I sporadically bumped into him when I swam ashore, but he seemed happy to be hanging out with his old friends and I didn't think much of it.

To be honest, I enjoyed having Hitrapia to myself. Over the last few months I'd spent so much time in Mark's company that it was a pleasant change and I assumed he felt the same way, so everything was hunky-dory.

After nearly three weeks of absence from Hitrapia, Mark invited me to jump aboard the tourist boat one afternoon for a free sunset tour to view the caves and beautiful beaches on the north coast of Mallorca. I happily joined him on the cruise boat and helped to prepare the food for the punters, distributing drinks whenever people were running dry. Mark was on top form as we ripped the piss out of each other, as usual, and it seemed as if everything was fine between us. I returned to Hitrapia that night on my own and while enjoying some music Ronny had recommended and the bottle of wine Yves had dropped off as my prize for winning our chess tournament, I was overwhelmingly happy and content. As I sat contemplating my life aboard, a fundamental truth embedded itself in my mind.

My life was remarkable, and as long as I remained positive and took the best out of every situation, it always would be. Every thought, action and experience I'd had up to that point had culminated in making me, me, and I liked the result. I knew I was far from perfect, but the majority of me was good and I was satisfied in the knowledge that I would make a positive contribution to the world.

I fell asleep that night a contented man, but as I've come to realise, when something seems too good to be true, then it normally is.

The next morning, I was awoken by Mark clambering back onto Hitrapia.

'We need to talk mate,' he stated as he handed me a cold beer.

'What's up?' I replied through a yawn. 'This is a bit early for alcohol.'

'Let's chat in the sun, I'm afraid I've got some bad news,' he said as he climbed out of the saloon and sat on the rail gazing out over the sea.

My heart skipped a beat. My immediate thought was that something had happened with his father, Laurie, who was battling cancer.

'This sounds ominous bro, has this got something to do with your dad?'

'Well, yes and no, he's fine but ... erm, there's no easy way to say this. I've been mulling it over for ages now and I've come to a decision.'

'Well spit it out then, the suspense is killing me,' I joked, trying to lighten the mood. I had no idea of the bombshell Mark was about to drop on me.

'I'm sorry mate, but I don't want to do this anymore.'

'Do what anymore?'

'This,' he said, as he swept a hand from the bow to the stern of Hitrapia, 'living on a little boat without any money. I'm not enjoying it anymore.'

He lifted the beer can to his mouth and almost drained it.

I was shocked. We hadn't seen much of each other lately but never in my worst nightmares would I have thought up this scenario.

'You must be joking,' I uttered in complete denial.

Mark just shrugged his shoulders, shook his head and looked forlornly out to sea. He had no words.

'You want to give up, you want to quit?'

Silence.

'But we've only just started mate, we haven't even left the Med yet.'

He looked up, drained the dregs from his beer and wiped his lips. 'Yip, that's kind of the point, Daz, I'm out of money and we've barely even started. You've already lent me two grand and the jobs I'll get sailing around the world, if they pay anything like this tourist boat gig, are never going to be enough.'

I shook my head as I spoke. 'But we've already booked flights back home for the summer so that you can tile for three months and get back on track. It's not like you don't have access to cash,' I responded in an attempt to bargain with him, 'you've got tens of thousands of pounds in equity in your house.'

'It's not just the money,' he said, 'I don't feel right about leaving when my dad's sick and I miss having a community around me. I miss my friends and my family.'

I didn't feel the need to mention that he was surrounded by an amazing community of fellow cruisers, if only he made an effort to get to know them. Laurie had been ill long before we'd bought the boat and was a hundred per cent behind Mark following his dreams.

I couldn't believe what he had just said and my brain was doing summersaults. I had a hundred and one questions to ask him.

'Does your decision have anything to do with not enjoying living on the yacht with me? Be honest bro'.

I've got broad shoulders, I can take it,' I asked as I looked him square in the eyes.

'Not at all Daz,' he responded, 'I've had an amazing time sailing with you, but this constant financial insecurity is a nightmare. I want to sail, I want to own my own yacht, but next time it'll be with a whole lot of money in the bank.'

As we sat, side by side, our legs dangling above the water and elbows leaning on the rails, on OUR boat, we were both deflated but I was utterly dumbfounded.

All I could think of was the amount of time we'd spent working and planning for the trip. All the sacrifices we made, scrimping and saving, to get where we were. After all the fun and adventures we'd enjoyed together, Mark was buckling before we encountered any significant obstacles and everything was going up in smoke.

'I'm sorry mate,' he remarked in a conciliatory tone, 'we always knew it was a gamble and might not work out.'

Of course it was a gamble. It was a gamble to give up the security of well-paid jobs, but we had done that and it was behind us. I'd never thought about the voyage in those terms. To me it was simple, when you make a commitment, you're committed. I'm a man of my word and if I say I'm going to do something - like sail around the world - then I'll move heaven and earth to make that happen. Come what may, I'd stick it out until the job was done or it was impossible to make any more progress. Giving up just isn't in my vocabulary. I'd never have made the commitment with Mark if I'd thought for a second that he'd just chuck in the towel when times got tough. I'd always felt we were in it together, through thick and thin, and I was gutted to the depths of my soul that he'd let me down. One of my closest friends had failed me and it felt like a dagger through my heart. With nothing else to say, an uncomfortable silence fell between us, before Mark made a mumbled excuse about getting back to shore. He jumped on the tender he had borrowed and headed off, leaving me dazed and confused on deck.

I spent the next couple of days shell shocked in a fog of denial and unanswered questions.

This can't be happening, I thought, it's like a bad dream. What had I done to make Mark stop wanting to sail with me? I'd spent an amazing few weeks on my own, on our boat, living the dream in paradise, confirming to myself that this was precisely what I wanted from life, but Mark mysteriously arrived at the exact opposite conclusion. It just didn't make sense. How had I possibly misread the situation so badly?

The questions went on and on inside my head as I went through the angry stage. How could Mark do this to me? I'd made enormous sacrifices, surely he knew that. What kind of a friend drops his mate in the shit like that?

I got over the angry stage and, in all honesty, it didn't last more than a few days. As in any breakup, I was going through the stages of grief required to get over a loss and it didn't take me long to get to the penultimate stage - acceptance. Mark is a gentle soul and I knew he didn't have a malicious bone in his body. I had to admit to myself that it had been a brave decision to make on his part. Circumnavigating the globe had been his dream too, but if he was unhappy, it was better to know now than on the other side of the Atlantic. It must have been a terrible weight to carry around, knowing he was about to let his partner down. Don't get me wrong, I was still thoroughly disappointed, but I could empathise with his situation, and holding grudges doesn't get you anywhere in life.

After acceptance, there was only one stage left, that of hope. I wasn't ready to give up on my dream of sailing around the world and it was time to start fighting for that dream's survival. If there was one thing I'd learnt about owning a boat, it was that there were always setbacks. Nothing ever runs entirely to plan and it was pointless getting angry about a situation that was beyond my control. It would only hinder my ability to come up with a solution. I'd only been focusing on the worst-case scenario of not being able to continue this epic voyage and lifestyle, now I needed to concentrate all of my efforts and attention on coming up with a way to keep it going. I made peace with Mark and we sat down to talk through the practicalities.

Mark was in a difficult place because he reneged on our agreement and I believed I had the right to buy his half of the boat. He agreed, but there was a significant obstacle, apart from the money - I needed to find someone to replace him.

We both had jobs to go-to for the summer and we went our separate ways. I flew to Switzerland, back to my sailing instructor's gig at Institut Le Rosey on Lake Geneva with a couple of months to come up with a solution.

At first, I telephoned anybody who I thought might be interested in owning a boat and sailing around the world. I used every ounce of my selling skills to cajole suitable candidates, but there were no takers. Then I changed tack and called on all my wealthy friends to see if they'd want to invest in a boat. I explained we could use it for charters and they'd get their money back within three years. They must have sensed my desperation and all politely yet sensibly refused the deal. I could feel my dream slipping away. One afternoon, as we cruised on Lake Geneva, I discussed my problem with another sailing instructor. Tom was sitting back and relaxing while I sailed the yacht on my own when he made an astute observation.

'You're more than capable of sailing a boat on your own. Why don't you just go solo bro?'

Tom's suggestion slowly sunk in. My dream of sailing around the world had been so interwoven with Mark that I'd always seen it as a two-man job. I had never even considered the adventure in any other terms, but the more I thought about it, the more it made sense. With a few minor adjustments to the boat, I could set her up for solo sailing.

It would be tough, but I'd already spent all that time and money getting to know Hitrapia intimately and knew it was possible. It would be a scary step to make on my own, but I was confident in my sailing abilities. There was one sticking point though: where would I find the money to buy Mark out? I didn't have nearly enough cash in the bank, but with a glimmer of hope again, I racked my brain for a solution. The next morning, I called my brother, Craig, and after taking a deep breath, I explained what I had in mind. Years before, Craig and I had bought a family home in England to enable my mother and grandmother the opportunity to move back to the United Kingdom, the place of their birth. Worried about their safety in South Africa as the political situation continued to deteriorate, we'd combined our resources and bought a big, four-bedroom house for us all to live in. Now that I'd gone sailing and my brother had remarried and moved out, the house was far too big for just my mum and gran and we'd been discussing downsizing for a while.

'Do you reckon we can sell the house? Otherwise, my dream is over.'

He pondered my question for a second, 'No worries little bro,' he said, 'but it could take years to sell. The housing market's dead at present.'

That's what I was afraid he'd say and my heart sank.

'I'll put the house up for sale immediately, but I may have a short-term solution. Let me speak to Eve (his wife) and I'll call you back in a bit.'

Craig rang me back three hours later with good news. He was willing to cash in all his investments and he'd also spoken to mum who'd lend me her savings too. They were both happy to wait until the house was sold to be repaid. I couldn't believe their generosity and how quickly my family had acted to preserve my dream. We went over the figures, but even with all the money combined, I was still four thousand pounds short on the repurchase price we had agreed upon, but Mark was gracious enough to take what money I could scramble together and agreed to let me pay the final instalment once the house was sold.

It had been an emotional rollercoaster and many a sleepless night, but my family had come through for me and it just goes to show that blood is always thicker than water.

With my finances in order, I returned to Mallorca after two months in Switzerland where Mark and I met up on Hitrapia. Lewis acted as Mark's witness as he signed his half of the boat over to me and Ronny acted as my witness as I countersigned in confirmation of the sale. My brother transferred the money into Mark's account and we all shook hands. The deal was done. Even though it was a business transaction, it was difficult for me to separate my emotions from the proceedings and the atmosphere felt strained. Mark and I had been through so much together and it was such a sad way for us to part company.

He collected his belongings from the boat, packed them in Lewis's van and our divorce was complete. All except for the four grand I would pay him in due course as soon as I had access to my house fund.

In for a penny, in for a pound, I thought. Now I was totally committed and everything I had was invested in Hitrapia. There was no going back and as I walked around a yacht I now owned outright, a beaming smile pulled across my face. I had fallen in love with her all over again. She was mine… all mine.

Ronny helped me install all the modifications I needed to turn Hitrapia into a single-handed vessel. He kept me company too as I got used to being 'single' again. Initially, the boat felt empty without Mark, as he'd been such an integral part of the adventure from the very start. I'd miss his company and unique brand of humour, but it is what it is. I was a wingman down, so it was time to learn how to fly solo. After a final beer with Ronny and a quick spin around the harbour to wave goodbye to my cruising friends, it was time to set off on the next chapter of my sailing odyssey.

Chapter 12

Going solo

Setting off from Mallorca was my first solo yacht sailing experience and the prospect was a daunting one. I'd sailed hundreds of times on my own but sailing a little four-metre dinghy on a freshwater lake within sight of land, isn't quite the same thing as setting out on a sea voyage all on your own.

I must admit that I was a little nervous as I pulled up the anchor by hand, wondering what I was truly getting myself into. In theory, solo sailing is the same as regular sailing, but with one fundamental difference - you're on your own. This may seem self-evident, but not only does it change the playing field, it changes the entire game. With somebody else on board, there's an extra set of hands, eyes and ears available to help out when needed. Issues that you don't see, hear or even think about are often taken care of by your crew before they become a problem. This allows you to concentrate on your specific jobs like steering or anchoring. It's especially helpful to have crew when conditions veer towards the windier side of the spectrum as things tend to go wrong that much quicker.

But when you are solo sailing, there is no buffer between you and a poor decision. You do everything yourself and any margin for error evaporates. To mitigate the many chances for mayhem, you have to think through the exact order of operations for each manoeuvre and practise them until it becomes second nature. With nobody else to blame for any fuckups, the buck stops with you and it's a very steep learning curve.

With all this in mind, I set off for the next island westwards, Ibiza, the epicentre of the party universe. I was on my way to pick up Katie – not the one I´d met in Cephalonia but a different one. Katie and I had met at a music festival a couple of summers before and she was keen to experience a sea gypsy's way of life so for the nominal charge of thirty pounds a day I'd offered to take her sailing and show her the ropes. As I was now the sole owner of Hitrapia it was time to explore different revenue streams and my first foray into chartering, in the company of a gorgeous girl, seemed like a great place to start.

After a pleasant day's sailing, I practised solo anchoring in a deserted little bay on Mallorca's north coast that evening. After ten attempts I was confident I knew the sequence by heart and could manage the manoeuvre in a crowded harbour on my own. I anchored in another bay further down the coast the next night, just to make sure. With headwinds for most of the way. I also had to tack (zigzag) through the wind about a hundred times. This got me proficient at swiftly shifting the lines from one winch to its opposite counterpart as the foresail flipped from one side of the boat to the other, all the while steering the yacht with my back, knees, elbows and occasionally toes. A fun, yet technical skill to master and a bit like gymnastics, just a whole lot wetter.

The third day was my first solo open water crossing between the islands. I set off at lunchtime and didn't sleep for twenty-four hours and arrived safely the next day in another little cove. It was just me, my boat, the wind and sea and I loved every minute of it. On the final day, I made the short hop down to San Antonio on the west coast of Ibiza to complete my first, four-day solo sailing voyage. I was incredibly proud of my achievement and felt like an intrepid adventurer, finally in complete control of my own destiny. I would no longer have to make any compromises and could go wherever my heart desired.

I arrived to pick up Katie in good time, but not before first practising mooring Hitrapia a dozen times on a deserted dock. The other sailors in the harbour must have thought I was mad as I motored slowly past the wharf and attempted to lasso one of the giant cleats used for mooring yachts. Wailing like a banshee when I failed on my initial attempts but screaming even louder in excitement when I got the hang of it and stopped the boat perfectly. With those necessary skills mastered, Hitrapia now felt well and truly like she belonged to me.

I picked up Katie from the main pier with a precision display of single-handed mooring. Katie knew nothing about sailing, so she wasn't too impressed, but I felt like a god as I'd only mastered the skill half an hour earlier. She jumped on board and we set off on a voyage of discovery down to the beautiful little island of Formentera in the south.

Katie

Formentera is the smallest of the four major Balearic Islands, the other three being Mallorca, Menorca and Ibiza. It has been a popular destination for hippies since the '60s and the picturesque white beaches are full of nudists. Be warned, the first time you are confronted by a gaggle of German old-age pensioners, proudly displaying their boobs and other dangly bits, it may come as quite a big shock. Especially, if like me, you weren't aware it was a naturist park in the first place.

On our third day out, as we approached an expanse of crystal-clear water dotted with numerous other yachts fifty meters off the stunning white sands of Cala Savina, I shouted over to a piratical looking character. He was heavyset and in his mid-fifties, with a tanned, well-creased face from decades spent observing the ocean. One of those guys who exudes the aura of a man of the sea as he perched on the back of his boat, smoking a hand-rolled cigarette.

'Excuse me, sir. I have no idea where your anchor is. If you wouldn't mind pointing me to a clear spot, I'd greatly appreciate it.'

The gentleman in question stood up.

With a hearty roar, he shouted back, 'Good evening Capitano, that spot just about twenty meters over there would be the perfect place to drop your anchor. It's sand, with no rocks, and good holding.'

'Cheers mate, how much chain have you got down?' I enquired as we glided by.

'Thirty metres Capitano,' he replied with an enormous smile that stretched from ear to ear.

In an anchorage, the quickest way to make enemies is to drop your anchor over the top of somebody else's and drag it free. The reason for equal lengths of chain is in case the wind changes direction, then all the yachts swing in identical arcs and don't bump into each other.

'Excellent, I'll drop the same amount then,' I replied as I proceeded to anchor Hitrapia in an efficient yet as nonchalant a manner as possible, all too aware that I had an audience for the first time. The gods were smiling, and the anchor dug in the first time, all my practise had paid dividends.

'Time for a glass of wine then my dear?' I asked Katie.

'Yeah, that would be lovely, but I'm afraid we finished it all off last night. I'm gagging for a smoke too, but I'm out of tobacco.'

'Bollocks,' I said.

I looked over towards my new friend and had an idea.

'I can try and sort out some tobacco from our neighbour, then we can head ashore and get some fresh food and wine. Does that sound like a plan?'

'Perfect,' she replied.

I lowered the tender into the water and rowed over to our new neighbour.

'Permission to come aboard sir,' I enquired as I nudged my tender next to his hull.

'Permission granted young man. Can I interest you in a glass of red wine? I've just opened a bottle.'

He sounded like my type of guy and I warmed to him immediately.

I tied up the tender and clambered aboard. We shook hands and introduced ourselves. His name was Daniele and he was Italian. He'd sailed all over the world for thirty years and had lived on that boat for the past twenty. After five minutes chatting, he eloquently excused himself and wandered to the front of his yacht. I averted my eyes as he proceeded to piss over the bow into the water.

There was a boat flying a German flag parked less than twenty meters off his bow. As he urinated, he shouted to them, 'Muovi la tua cazzo di barca pezzo di merda!'

I know enough Italian to understand what he was saying, which roughly translates to, 'Move your fucking boat you piece of shit!'

He made his way back to the cockpit with a smile, 'Okay my friend, let's have another glass of wine.'

He ranted throughout the first bottle of red. 'Those fucking wankers dropped their anchor directly upwind from me this morning and have been slowly dragging backwards all day. They'll be on top of me by midnight,' he exclaimed.

Now I knew the reason why he was pissing in their general direction and shouting obscenities. I later found out he was infamously known as the 'Italian Pirate', apt to threaten any charter boat that decided to anchor too close to him.

'The only reason I allowed you onboard Capitano, is that you're the first sailor to have any manners in the last month. It's obvious you know what you're doing.'

I must admit my chest puffed out with pride at the compliment and at being called Captain, Daniele's nickname for me from that point onwards. I told him my name several times, but he never used it. We chatted away for about half an hour as we drained the last of the bottle and he was just about to open another one when Katie popped her head up from below Hitrapia's decks.

The Italian looked over and pointed. 'Your Bellissima lady friend has reappeared Capitano, would you like to invite her over?'

I shook my head, 'to be honest mate I only popped over to borrow some tobacco, Katie and I need to head ashore to pick up some supplies for tonight's meal.'

'Then you have a problem,' Daniele pointed out, 'it's a Sunday night. All the shops within miles from here are closed.

'Porca miseria,' I uttered in my limited vocabulary.

Daniele laughed out loud, 'ha, miserable pig, you speak good Italian Capitano.'

I shook my head, 'good…not at all, I only know the swear words.'

'That's good enough for me. Now, what do you need?'

'We're out of tobacco and wine, plus Katie is sick of eating the tinned food I have onboard. I hoped to cook her something with fresh ingredients tonight.'

'No problema Capitano, I'm Italian and all Italians cook. I have wine, tobacco and rum if you like. Please join me for the evening, you are both very welcome.'

I didn't know what to say so I offered a token refusal.

'I won't take no for an answer.'

'Thanks, Daniele. That's very kind of you, but I'd better ask the boss first.'

'Then do it,' he said, 'while I open the next bottle.'

As he reached for the corkscrew, I climbed back into the tender to fetch Katie, who needed no urging as she was hungry, thirsty and in need of some nicotine. Always up for an adventure, she jumped in and I rowed her back to the Italian's yacht.

As we climbed aboard, Daniele held out a hand and helped Katie up.

'First thing for a party is music, my friends. What do you like to listen to?'

I looked at Katie and shrugged my shoulders.

'Anything really,' she said.

'Well I have everything on tape, so sometimes it just takes a little while to find what I want to play,' Daniele remarked as he scrambled around in the ship's hold.

'Tapes' I thought as I caught a quizzical look on Katie's face. We must have misheard him, but no, seconds later Daniele reappeared with a cassette playing ghetto blaster manufactured some time way back in the '80s.

'Guys, this is Cazzo (dick or fuck in Italian),' he stated as he introduced us to his tape deck.

'Cazzo, these are our guests. You better behave yourself tonight Cazzito, or you know what happens,' he said as he waved an accusatory finger at the old machine. 'You will have to excuse Cazzo. He is old and useless, but he's all I've got,' he confided in us.

We had absolutely no idea what he was going on about, but we were soon to find out. He continued to chat to his tape player as if it were a member of his crew, a possible side effect of spending too much time on his own.

The music went on and Daniele started cooking until five minutes later, poor Cazzo began to screech as an ancient, stretched cassette tape got jammed.

'Oh, Cazzo! Vaffanculo!' Daniele cried as he slapped the machine and cursed for all he was worth until miraculously, the music started playing again.

'You see, he misbehaves. The only way to keep him playing is to beat him like a red-headed stepchild.'

Daniele chuckled as he headed back to the galley.

The rest of the evening proceeded in a similar vein. If the Italian Pirate wasn't cursing at the tape deck, then he was swearing at the boat out front, all the while telling us ridiculous stories of his adventures and plying us with delicious pasta and wine. By midnight both Katie and I were crying from laughing so much. It was late and time to head home, but not before inviting Daniele aboard Hitrapia for dinner the following evening to repay the favour.

We spent an exciting couple of days exploring Formentera during the day and being royally entertained by Daniele at night, but it was soon time to head back north to drop Katie off in San Antonio. Her brief holiday was at an end as she had to return to the 'real' world. As fate would have it, the very same day she departed, two of my good friends from South Africa, Taryn and Liz, arrived in Ibiza to celebrate their thirtieth birthdays. The Italian Pirate duly organised me a mooring from one of his mates, Fernando, for the minuscule charge of 10€ per day, a fraction of the price you can typically expect to pay in Ibiza. Fernando promised to watch over Hitrapia while I was away so I could go and party to my heart's content. With everything shipshape and the yacht attached to a robust mooring buoy, I hit the town to surprise the girls. They had no idea I was coming and I had no idea they'd brought twenty other people with them. I met them all at the Ocean Club in San Antonio to shrieks of delight and with such a large crew of party animals, it was going to be carnage, just the way I like it.

The Ocean Club is an outdoor party scene with banging music and several magnificent aquamarine swimming pools. It was crammed full of beautiful people, frolicking about in their swimwear and there were terrific live acrobatic displays, performed up in the sky, by dancers suspended from ribbons or attached to hot air balloons.

Partying at the Ocean Club with Nik

Every party in Ibiza is spectacular and each venue tries to outshine its rivals. It's not just an audio experience but a visual kaleidoscope of delight too. After the Ocean Club, our team of reprobates decided to hail some taxis, and we headed over to Bora Bora Beach on the other side of the island where we celebrated the sun going down in the true Ibizan style of dancing on some tables. Around midnight it was time to move on again and we all headed to Space

Nightclub. If you love to dance and you've never been to Ibiza, then you haven't really experienced the full might of the party scene. Ibiza is the Mecca of mega-clubs with capacity inside most venues of around five thousand people, but the biggest club, Privilege, holds ten thousand. The clubs are packed every night and host the best and most famous DJs in the world.

You can dance for twenty-four hours and keep on partying, day after day, as long as you have the stamina to keep going and bundles of cash as the mega-clubs' admittance charges and drink prices are extortionate. Fortunately, our group included some people with connections in the music industry, so we got free entry everywhere we went and the occasional free drink as well. It was a huge night out and we left Space at sunrise, heading back to the villa my friends had rented where we chilled out for a couple of hours, but by late afternoon the next party broke out. It was sundown by the time somebody announced that the pool party was over and time to head into Ibiza old town. We went for some cocktails and then hit the oldest and most beautiful club on the Island, Es Paradis.

Es Paradis is a magnificent club with an all-white interior and enormous natural gardens. It has an impressive amphitheatre, surrounded by marble columns, and each night they put on a very chic and glamorous show. There are few experiences in life better than the euphoric natural rush you get from fantastic music, played in a spectacular venue, while dancing with a bunch of your beautiful friends. I was in seventh heaven despite being almost out of energy. All good things must come to an end though and we stumbled out of the club at daybreak. There were only two of us left, me and an ex-elite soldier called Damo, literally the last two men standing.

Damo is a private security contractor who had recently arrived back from the desert of some far-flung war-torn country. Solidly built and as hard as nails, there aren't many people who can out-party me, but Damo was a definite heavyweight contender for the title. We wandered into a little shop, grabbed some beers and sat on the beach to chill.

'You're an absolute warrior mate, good effort,' I complimented him as we chinked our cans.

'So are you mate, so are you.'

We reminisced about how much fun we'd had together, both feeling a little re-energised by the rising sun, even though it had almost been two straight days of dancing and drinking. We had caught our second, third or perhaps even fourth wind, so I invited Damo back to Hitrapia as he'd never been on a yacht before. As we clambered aboard at 9 am, I heard some distant shouting and a thumping baseline.

'This place is ridiculous,' I exclaimed, 'Ibiza never sleeps.'

The shouting grew louder until I turned around and realised it was being directed at me.

'Hey, hey, what are you doing on that boat?' Fernando barked at me from his tender.

'Good morning Fernando, it's me, Daz. Remember, this is my boat?'

'Ah, welcome back my friend,' he waved in recognition, 'I didn't realise it was you. I thought somebody was trying to break in.'

'It's all good buddy, I really appreciate you looking after the boat though, fancy a beer?'

'Sure, why not?' he said, 'Daniele the Pirate has just sailed in and we are having a rave on that big catamaran over there. Do you and your friend still want to party?'

I gazed over at Damo with a questioning look.

'Hell yeah,' he stated, 'I didn't fly all the way from the Middle East to go to bed. Sleep when you're dead!'

That settled it. We jumped into Fernando's tender with a bag of booze filled from my fridge and ventured to yet another party. After the rave aboard the catamaran, I invited a dozen people back to Hitrapia for an after-party, but all the revelry had gotten the better of me and I began to wane. Even Damo had bailed, which was fair enough as he had outlasted all the others and still had to get back to his villa. My boat was now full of people I didn't know except for the Italian Pirate and Fernando.

'You're looking tired Capitano, you need to sleep,' he stated.

And that was it. Daniele saw I was exhausted, not enjoying myself anymore and called a halt to the party.

'Vámonos!' He bellowed, shooing everyone off Hitrapia in minutes. We finished off our last rum and coke together and then he headed off too, leaving me in the sweet embrace of silence. I had survived in that den of iniquity for more hours than I cared to remember, and it was high time I got some sleep.

My time in Ibiza was drawing to a close and it took me a couple of days to recover after the relentless partying. I also needed to prepare myself mentally for the upcoming sail through the Strait of Gibraltar. After stocking up on provision and getting some well-deserved rest, I felt ready for the challenge. Daniele popped over to say a final goodbye and almost crushed me in a bear hug. He is one of the most generous and outrageous sailors I've ever had the privilege of meeting and I hope he is still screaming at Cazzo for being useless, or anybody stupid enough to anchor anywhere near him. Unless, of course, you have the manners to ask him courteously first, then he'd take the shirt off his back to help you out.

It was a short sail to Spain's mainland and I made my way down the coast. There aren´t a huge amount of protected anchorages along the way, so I had to make some overnight passages to find safe bays to bunker down in, but after my sleep deprivation training in Ibiza, staying awake overnight had become child's play.

The Strait of Gibraltar is the narrow band of water, only 7.7 nautical miles wide at its narrowest point, separating Gibraltar (which belongs to Britain) and Peninsular Spain in Europe from Morocco and Ceuta (which belongs to Spain), in Africa.

With millions of tons of water flowing in and out of the Mediterranean, it's a tricky place to sail due to its powerful currents. It's imperative to time your sailing transit with an outgoing tide, but more importantly, to have the wind behind you so that you're not beating into it. The wind switched to the east and I had a clear twenty-four-hour weather window, so I went for it. The Strait can be a formidable adversary, with the combination of changing winds and tides, but to make matters worse, it also happens to be one of the busiest shipping lanes in the world. With hundreds of commercial vessels shipping their goods through the narrow channel, it's a daunting prospect and even more so when you're entirely on your own. It turned out that I wasn't on my own though as I had company for the entire eight-hour passage from my very own aquatic angels.

As I began my transit through the Strait, I was feeling vulnerable in my little boat, surrounded by huge tankers charging along–four times faster than me. I also felt emotional about leaving the Mediterranean Sea and finally reaching the Atlantic Ocean.

At the point when I felt most alone and isolated, the first pod of dolphins arrived. There is nothing quite as cheering to a troubled soul as seeing these majestic creatures, full of mischief and play, frolicking in the bow wave of the boat as they catch a free ride.

With a far too human stare, they swam on their sides and peered up at me while they chatted away in their high-pitched squeaks and squeals. With Hitrapia sailing well under Manny the Monitor's excellent steerage, I only had to change course twice to pass two large ships safely. The rest of the time I sat on the bow, talking away to my new friends in the water as I kept a wary eye on all the boat traffic around me. They seemed to love the company too and I told them all how beautiful they were as they streaked through the shimmering water. As one pod tired of escorting me and left, another pod arrived and took over the patrol. It was as if they were passing a baton from one to another in a relay as they guided me onwards. In the end, I passed through the Strait with ease and two days later I arrived in the fateful little bay of Baleeira, in Sagres, on the southwestern tip of Portugal and you already know about the havoc that followed. My eyes mist up every time I think of my first, and last, ocean voyage with Hitrapia in the company of those incredible dolphins.

BOOK 2

Chapter 1

Round two

It was precisely a year to the day I'd been shipwrecked in Portugal. I was back in the UK, visiting my mum and I'd just finished a Skype interview with a skipper intending to sail around the world. He was looking for crew to help him sail from Las Palmas in the Canary Islands all the way to Australia on the World ARC (Atlantic Rally for Cruisers) and I'd got the gig.
I ran into the kitchen, picked my Mum up and spun her around in the air.
'Woohoo! I'm going back to sea,' I squealed in delight, 'and this time I'm going to make it all the way around the world!'

The two weeks post shipwreck in Portugal was a traumatic experience. As well as having to deal with the emotional turmoil of losing my beautiful boat, there was also the uncertainty of my future. My whole world had been turned upside down and I did the

only thing I could to try and forget the torment and pain - I buried myself in work.
From sunrise to sunset, I grafted like a Trojan, trying to salvage my belongings and anything else of value not yet destroyed by the ocean as everything I owned in the world got pounded twice a day by the incoming tide. It was initially a mad dash to get as much of my gear out of the wreckage as possible and stashed on higher ground. Within two days of Pablo informing me that Hitrapia was lost, the beach looked like a refugee camp, with my pitched tent and salt-encrusted possessions strewn everywhere above the tide's high waterline.
Sails, surfboards, clothes, books, tools, spares and all the electronics that hadn't been submerged in seawater; everything had to be removed. Once I saved what I could from the sea, I trudged it the two hundred metres along the beach to a warehouse the local boatyard owner had lent me for storage. There I dumped the damp contents of what was left of my life on the workshop's oily concrete floor. I then painstakingly washed each item with freshwater and hung everything out to dry. After each exhausting day I retired to my tent on the beach, thirty metres from the shipwreck, only to be woken up most nights as nefarious locals descended onto the carcass of Hitrapia and tried to plunder whatever was left behind. I chased them off, knowing they'd be back again and almost lost my self-control one morning when I woke up to see two young children clambering all over the wreck while their parents stood by laughing.
'What do you think this is?' I screamed at the adults, 'A fucking jungle gym!'

They didn't understand a word I said, but they got the message loud and clear and beat a hasty retreat. My beautiful boat turned into a kid's play park; their disrespect galled me for days.

It was a recurring nightmare that continued until I'd stripped the boat bare. Other than my unwelcome late-night visitors, I was surrounded throughout the experience by a bunch of amazing friends in Sagres, old and new, who helped me out immeasurably.

Jesus, Didier, Sylvia, Concha, Marta and Michaël, to name just a few. I will never be able to thank them enough for their varied assistance as I wouldn't have coped without their help. After two weeks John, the Dutch insurance surveyor who had made himself indispensable by sorting out the attempted salvage effort, organised a thirty-ton crusher. It rolled onto the beach, destroyed Hitrapia in a matter of hours and piled the mangled wreckage into two skips on the beach. The giant metal dustbins were then loaded onto the back of a truck and that was that. An ignoble end to what had once been a vessel of sublime beauty and infinite potential.

It was fortunate for me that it was a clear case of negligence on behalf of the port authority who'd rented me their mooring. They hadn't serviced the buoy for years and the chain had snapped, resulting in the total loss of my yacht. They were therefore liable for all the damages incurred.

My insurance company paid out within a month of the accident and I once again became cash-rich but boat-poor - straight back to square one. After the accident I was emotionally exhausted as it felt like my soul had been ripped from my body and I decided to get as far away from yachts as possible. I needed space

and time to clear my head because losing Hitrapia felt like a bereavement. Yet, I still felt drawn to water. I still loved the ocean and didn't hold it at all accountable for the calamity that had befallen me. It had been human error, pure and painfully simple.
I decided to skip the European winter and headed to Australasia, spending a month in Sydney visiting my adopted brother Craig Arnold. He’s an extraordinary character and one of the most positive people I've ever met - just the kind of person I needed to be around to help mend my broken heart. I then headed over to New Zealand, bought a small people carrier and converted it into a camper van. I lost myself in the mystic wilds of the North and South Islands of Aotearoa, 'The land of the long white cloud,' for five blissful months. From Auckland, I made my way down the coast, surfing and camping on untouched beaches all the way to the southern fjords and Milford Sound. From lush, fertile vineyards to the soaring mountains known as the Southern Alps, New Zealand has some of the most spectacular scenery I've ever seen. All of this beauty is compressed into two little islands, filled with a population that is so friendly, it's almost offensive. It is one of the most beautiful and unspoilt places I've ever had the privilege of exploring and just the salve I needed for my devastated soul.
During this time the pain of losing my yacht lessened, but at the back of my mind there was an unshakeable feeling that I still had unfinished business to attend to. No matter how hard I tried, the thought was always with me that I'd started, but not completed, the adventure I had planned and dreamed of for fifteen years. My shattered vision of sailing around the world would forever remain on that beach in Portugal unless

I did something about it. I pondered these questions late at night as I lay in my camper van staring at the Southern Hemisphere's stars. What kind of person would I be if I just gave up on my dream? Would I grow old and have regrets about what might have been? Could I look at myself in the mirror, knowing that I'd failed in my quest? There were times when I'd try and convince myself to give up on the idea, thinking it was stupid, dangerous and expensive. Then I'd recall my father's little lectures when I was younger. One, in particular, sprang to mind, and his form would come to me as clear as day. I could envisage this big, towering man, the wrinkles on his forehead pinched ever closer together as he concentrated, his words floating into my mind as if he were talking to me from the afterlife. 'A promise is a promise Darroch, if you say you're going to do something, then you get it done. No matter what happens, you must always be a man of your word.' I couldn't shake those words. My father was right.

I had promised myself I was going to sail around the world, so I put any thoughts of quitting out of my mind. I ventured back to Europe when it got too cold in the Southern Hemisphere and did my normal two months Swiss summer school stint. By the end of summer I'd had enough time to lick my wounds and it was time to get back to sea. I thought long and hard about buying another yacht, but my mind kept going back to a conversation I'd had with Alan on my first transatlantic crossing. When I mentioned I was going to buy a boat and sail around the world, he'd laughed out loud.

'Don't be stupid boy, sail other people's yachts, it's much cheaper.'
The more I thought about it, the more I realised how much sense it made. I didn't have a limitless budget and knew from experience how expensive yachts could be. It was time to try a different tack. I decided to crew on other people's boats and attempt to sail around the world that way instead.
I flew into Las Palmas at the beginning of November 2015, laden down with sixty kilograms of luggage. You know you've brought too much stuff when the airline charges you more for your second bag than they did for your flight and first bag combined, but the circumnavigation would take in all the seasons, so I packed for every eventuality.
Las Palmas felt familiar as it had only been three years since I first landed there in search of a yacht to take me across the Atlantic, but I was wiser and way more experienced than back then. One thing hadn't changed though - adrenalin still coursed through my veins at the thought of setting out to sea again. Sailing under an unknown captain would be a challenging experience as I'd spent eighteen months as the skipper of my own boat, but it was a trade-off I'd just have to get used to.
Bobby, the owner and skipper of my new boat, met me on the dock next to Free Spirit. She was a Jeaunneau Sun Odyssey 54DS and his pride and joy. Bobby was a short, jovial, middle-aged character of medium build who exuded a charisma and vitality that was quite endearing. He welcomed me aboard and introduced me to the other two crew members, Joern and Michael, who'd arrived earlier in the week and were busy with various jobs. After a quick

handshake, I stowed my belongings in my cabin and went straight to work. With only five days until the start of the rally, there were still a ton of jobs to complete before the yacht was ready for an ocean crossing.

We all worked extremely hard during the daylight hours, then settled down to some proper drinking in the evenings. It's imperative to get to know the people you're about to go sailing with before you set off on a voyage, and the surest route to cementing these critical relationships, in the shortest possible time, is to lubricate conversations with a lot of alcohol.

Even though Free Spirit was a fifty-four-foot yacht, it was still a small space for four people to live in for almost three weeks at sea, so we all put in a big effort to bond as a team. Joern, a big chunk of a Swiss guy, had vast amounts of sailing experience. A robust and dependable character, I was happy he was onboard as it's always comforting to know you're heading out to sea with at least one other person who can really handle themselves when the shit hits the fan. Michael, on the other hand, was a retired doctor and not particularly experienced in sailing matters, other than in the art of astronavigation. His primary reason for the voyage was to use his sextant - a navigational instrument measuring the angular distance between two objects - to calculate our position on the ocean from the sun and stars. This was great news for me. Astronavigation was a nautical skill I'd been dying to understand yet I hadn't sailed with anybody capable or willing to teach it to me. Michael seemed more than happy to pass on his knowledge of this arcane art, so I was doubly excited about the upcoming crossing. Bobby was an interesting one. Although not an experienced skipper, he was intelligent and he was knowledgeable about the theoretical side of sailing and focused on problem-solving. He also wasn't averse to spending his money on equipment required for the trip. Unless you've owned a boat, you won't understand how expensive it is to run one - and the bigger the boat, the bigger the problems and the hungrier the black hole for your hard-earned cash gets. Bobby didn't cut any corners with regard to expenses on the yacht, and after the first few days I developed a healthy respect for his organisational abilities.

Through the loss of litres of blood, sweat and tears we got the boat ready in time for the official start of the ARC+ (the Atlantic Rally for Cruisers that goes via the Cape Verde Islands) with an hour to spare.

We manoeuvred well and hit the start line of the rally in the top five out of a fleet of over sixty yachts and it became immediately apparent that Bobby was in it to win it. It was definitely a race for him and not the easy-going rally it was initially intended to be. The fundamental difference between these two approaches to sailing is that a racer's mindset is always to push the boat to its limit for extra speed. This means more sail up in stronger winds, for longer periods of time, increasing the level of risk of an accident for both the yacht and her crew.

On the other hand, a cruiser's mindset is to mitigate as much of the inherent risk in sailing as possible, by not straining the boat or placing unnecessary demands on the crew. This means a far more conservative approach where safety trumps speed every time. These two opposing approaches to a long ocean passage put Bobby and me at odds with each other from the start. I love taking risks and going to ridiculous lengths to scare myself half to death, just not when I'm sailing. When I sail, I am completely risk averse. The sea is such a treacherous environment that I see no need to make it any more dangerous than it already is, especially when crossing oceans where you can be weeks away from any kind of assistance if things go wrong.

During the first couple of days, I frequently advocated reefing the sails early and dropping the spinnaker (the vast, billowing sail that is flown from the bow of the boat) at the first sign of inclement weather, but Bobby preferred to push on until the last possible moment.
I felt this was reckless and endangered us all. Still, we arrived safely in Mindelo after six days without any catastrophes. Mindelo is the port city on São Vicente, in the volcanic archipelago of Cape Verde, situated off the west coast of Africa. It's made up of colourful colonial houses set against a backdrop of low-lying rugged mountains. A quaint little place but in need of some tender loving care as it is dirt poor and run down.
We only had a couple of days to explore this vibrant little city that's famous for its Creole Afro-Portuguese cultural mix. Cape Verde was first colonised by the Portuguese in the fifteenth century and used as a base for their slave trade. With the mingling of many different ethnic groups, it's not uncommon to see beautiful, dark-skinned women with blond hair and piercing blue eyes or light-skinned women sporting afros. I managed to buy some decent fishing lures and we visited a couple of the nearby islands. However, it

was only a short stopover before we headed out to sea again.

As the voyage progressed we only encountered the occasional light squall during the day and nothing adverse at night so my conservative outlook started to fall on deaf ears. At the beginning of the trip we agreed to put one reef in the mainsail before sundown every night, but this fell by the wayside as we found ourselves sitting in third position in our race class after ten days at sea. The old sailing adage holds that there can only be one skipper onboard, so I had to bite my tongue and accept that my advice, at times, was blatantly ignored. It was Bobby's boat; he was the captain and the final decision was always going to be his.

It was around midnight on the tenth night and I was off watch and sound asleep in my cabin when I was woken up by a change in the rhythm of the boat. It's incredible how attuned you become to your environment after spending some time at sea and I'd immediately sensed the boat's acceleration. Seconds later I heard Joern shouting down the companionway, 'Daz, get up here quick!'

Remember to read Books 2 & 3
The World's my Oyster Trilogy
AVAILABLE ON AMAZON
The World's my Oyster
Book 2
A tale of one man's dream to sail around the globe
Daz Tait
The World's my Oyster
Book 3
A tale of one man's dream to sail around the globe
Daz Tait

Printed in Great Britain
by Amazon

51865486R00111